"We expect lies to come as attacks, not gentle whispers of self-talk. These weeds often grow unnoticed in spaces where the reality of God—who He is, who He says we are, and what He has called us to be and do—has simply been forgotten. The antidote to lies is always truth. John Stange gently reminds us of much that we've forgotten and encourages us to pay closer attention to what we allow to take up residence in our minds."

—TANYA DENNIS, writer, Bible teacher, and contributing author to the NIV Bible for Women

"As a small child, I had the impression that God was big, harsh, and condescending to the insignificant humans He had created. It took years to learn of God's goodness and His desire for us to live with joy and victory. John's personalized stories remind us that God is our kind, generous, and giving heavenly Father. As a father myself, I eagerly anticipated these daily biblical truths of God that speak to us of the characteristics I want to model to my own children."

—DAN MILLER, author of 48 Days to the Work You Love and host of the 48 Days podcast

"We live in a world where we are constantly bombarded with distracting and discouraging messages. Dwell on These Things is a simple, fresh approach to help you develop the mind of Christ. If you're ready to grow in your faith and confidence, this book is for you!"

—KENT SANDERS, author of The Artist's Suitcase: 26 Essentials for the Creative Journey and ghostwriter

"As a Christian, I am tempted to see a book on self-talk and think, *Yeah, I already know this,* but *Dwell on These Things* is unique. Through thirty-one daily readings, Stange challenges us to go beyond the mere knowledge of Scripture and to actually dwell on it to change our beliefs. Challenge accepted! By utilizing mindful self-talk straight from the Word of God, we can replace the lies we've been teaching ourselves to believe with the truths we were meant to embrace. This is a life-transformational read to start each day with—over and over again!"

—RENEE VIDOR, founder of the Winner's Circle and author of *Measuring Up: How to WIN in a World of Comparison*

"It was later in my life when I found myself having a deeper relationship with God in my spiritual walk. It has taken a lot of inner reflection, study, and prayer to make sense of it all. In reading *Dwell on These Things,* I resonated with John's stories and saw part of my own journey in how he describes his path. I also appreciate the 'Dwell on This' sections that give usable thoughts to reflect on throughout the day, giving me a deeper meaning to life's journey."

—CHAD JEFFERS, author, professor, multi-instrumentalist for Grammy Award–winning artist Carrie Underwood, and real estate agent at Compass

"Thought strengthening! In this timely book, John Stange delivers a transparent plan that will inspire you to preach God's Word through your own self-talk. Dwelling on these lessons will transform your perspective, giving you freedom from the labels given to you by relentless worldly lies."

—BEE EVANS, founder of EMBLDN Label and host of *Tear Out the Tags* podcast

"Through relatable stories and his own experiences, John helps us identify false narratives and presents scriptural truths our hearts so desperately need. He focuses on the foundation of who God is and who He is for us. The daily 'Dwell on This' statements have been a powerful tool to internalize God's truths each morning. *Dwell on These Things* is a refreshing read for anyone wanting to deepen their connection with God."

—LINDSAY MAY, founder of the Truly Co and publisher of *Truly* magazine

"Oh no, another devotional book! Yes, it is, but this is different . . . no, really! Each day starts with a Scripture verse and ends with practical application. In between are personal, transparent stories from real life that make the devotional practical, helpful, and fun to read. You may even find yourself peeking at tomorrow's chapter! If our physical bodies reveal what we eat, our spirits certainly reflect what we think on. In *Dwell on These Things*, John Stange gives us some real spiritual food."

—TIM MADEIRA, cohost of *Wake Up Right* and general manager of WRGN Radio

"Do you talk to yourself like God talks to you? This was the question that kept going through my mind as I read John's new book. His insights brought tears to my eyes as I realized once again that we are often our own worst enemy. If you want to hear God's voice more clearly and bring more peace into your life, make *Dwell on These Things* your daily companion."

—SADIE KOLVES, author of *Anything Is Possible*

DWELL ON THESE THINGS

DWELL ON
THESE THINGS

A Thirty-One-Day Challenge
to Talk to Yourself Like God
Talks to You

JOHN STANGE

WATERBROOK

Published in the United States by WaterBrook, an imprint of Random House, a division of Penguin Random House LLC.

WATERBROOK® and its deer colophon are registered trademarks of Penguin Random House LLC.

Library of Congress Cataloging-in-Publication Data
Names: Stange, John, author.
Title: Dwell on these things : a thirty-one-day challenge to talk to yourself like God talks to you / John Stange.
Description: First edition. | Colorado Springs : WaterBrook, 2021.
Identifiers: LCCN 2020035542 | ISBN 9780593193297 (trade paperback) | ISBN 9780593193303 (ebook)
Subjects: LCSH: Identity (Psychology)—Religious aspects—Christianity. | Self-talk—Religious aspects—Christianity.
Classification: LCC BV4509.5 .S735 2021 | DDC 248.4—dc23
LC record available at https://lccn.loc.gov/2020035542

Printed in the United States of America on acid-free paper

waterbrookmultnomah.com

9 8 7 6 5 4 3 2 1

First Edition

Interior book design by Diane Hobbing

SPECIAL SALES Most WaterBrook books are available at special quantity discounts when purchased in bulk by corporations, organizations, and special-interest groups. Custom imprinting or excerpting can also be done to fit special needs. For information, please email specialmarketscms@penguinrandomhouse.com.

This book is dedicated to you if you have ever filled your mind with negative self-talk, made the mistake of preaching a false gospel to your heart, or struggled to see yourself from God's perspective.

Jesus is the solution.

Finally brothers and sisters, whatever is true, whatever is honorable, whatever is just, whatever is pure, whatever is lovely, whatever is commendable—if there is any moral excellence and if there is anything praiseworthy—dwell on these things.

—Philippians 4:8, CSB

CONTENTS

Introduction   xi

DAY 1: You are loved more deeply than you realize.   3

DAY 2: Walk by faith rather than by sight to experience greater joy.   9

DAY 3: Let your heart be ruled by the peace of Christ.   16

DAY 4: Any trial can be an occasion for joy.   22

DAY 5: Dwell on God's kindness toward you.   29

DAY 6: Give grace to those around you.   35

DAY 7: You can rely on God's unconditional love.   41

DAY 8: Cast your anxiety on God instead of bearing the
         weight yourself.   47

DAY 9: Choose not to be easily provoked by others.   53

DAY 10: Listen to those who love you enough to tell you the truth.   59

DAY 11: Make the most of your privilege to repent.   64

DAY 12: God's goodness and mercy are pursuing you.   70

DAY 13: You can take refuge in God.   75

DAY 14: God wipes your slate clean.   81

DAY 15: The Lord will keep His promises to you.   87

DAY 16: Today is a great day to display the gentleness of Christ.   93

DAY 17: Be respectful, even if you disagree.   100

DAY 18: Unhealthy habits and desires don't need to control you.   107

DAY 19: Don't adopt this world's depressive outlook as your own.   113

DAY 20: The Lord hears your cry for mercy.   120

DAY 21: Don't let fear of others hold you back from
         God's purpose for your life.   127

DAY 22: Pray for those who have intentionally hurt you.   134

DAY 23: Don't let your heart be troubled.   141

DAY 24: The dominant voice your heart hears should not be
         one of condemnation.   148

DAY 25: There is greater joy in giving than in consuming.   154

DAY 26: The Lord delights in you when you work and
         when you rest.   161

DAY 27: Trade your fears for confidence in God.   167

DAY 28: Focus on issues that truly matter.   174

DAY 29: Value listening as much as you value speaking.   180

DAY 30: The issues that weigh you down today won't weigh
         you down forever.   187

DAY 31: You can trust God's timing to be perfect.   193

         Acknowledgments   199

INTRODUCTION

You've been talking to yourself today. In fact, you've been talking to yourself your entire life. You talk to yourself when you wake up each morning, when you're driving, when you're trying to fall asleep at night, and every moment in between. You even talk to yourself when other people are trying to talk to you. And you're not alone. We're all talking to ourselves, but we're not all saying—or hearing—the same things.

During the course of your life, you've probably spent many hours listening to lessons delivered by teachers, lectures given by professors, and sermons shared by pastors. I'm sure the information shared was helpful, but these people had only limited opportunities to speak to you. You have far greater opportunities to talk to yourself than they have. In fact, no one else will have the opportunity to teach, lecture, or preach to you more than you will.

So, what are you telling yourself?

What does your mind dwell on?

Would you talk to someone else the way you talk to yourself?

What messages are you preaching to your heart?

There are all sorts of messages being aimed at our hearts and minds each day. Some of these messages are true and helpful; others are hurtful, destructive, and out of line with the message God wants us to understand and embrace. What messages are you choosing to believe and repeat to yourself? When you first saw your reflection in the mirror this morning, what did your internal conversation sound like? Did you speak a message of hope to your heart or a diatribe of defeat?

What do you tell yourself when you experience physical pain, disappointment, or betrayal?

Is the message you preach to your heart reminding you of the goodness of God, or is the message you're pounding into your heart fostering a sense of discouragement and depression?

If you could see God, face to face, standing right in front of you, what do you think He would say to you? Do you think the message He would want to share with you would be similar to what you've been telling yourself, or would it be drastically different?

God does communicate with us. During the course of history, He has spoken to people in different ways. To some, He spoke audibly. To others, He spoke in dreams and visions. He spoke to His people through prophets. He spoke to us through His Son, Jesus Christ. He speaks to our hearts through His Spirit as He comforts, convicts, and imparts wisdom. And He has given us His Word, the Bible.

In this current day, we have greater access to God's Word than any generation that has come before us. But for many of us, it can be far too easy to take that access for granted. We're so used to being able to read it and study it whenever we want that we can begin treating it like an unvalued resource. This is emotionally and spiritually tragic.

If we minimize the Word of God, we'll persist in ignorance.

If we minimize the Word of God, we'll gradually adopt false beliefs.

If we minimize the Word of God, we'll give the devil a foothold in our minds.

And the icing on the cake is that we'll begin preaching a message to our hearts that's the exact opposite of the truth of the gospel. Have you already started to notice this in your own life? If so, would you like to interrupt this pattern and begin replacing the lies you've mistakenly believed with the truth?

Luke 4 tells us that the Holy Spirit led Jesus into the wilderness, where He remained for forty days. During that time, the devil repeatedly tempted Jesus. He tried to make Jesus submit to him. He tried to persuade Jesus to adopt a worldly mindset. He tried to influence Jesus to idolize temporary comforts, and he even had the audacity to try to make Jesus worship him. But Jesus didn't give in to the devil's schemes. He resisted him, and He exposed the ways the devil was distorting and misrepresenting the truth. Jesus did this by quoting the Word of God:

> Jesus answered him, "It is written, 'Man shall not live by bread alone.'" (verse 4)

> Jesus answered him, "It is written,
>   'You shall worship the Lord your God,
>   and him only shall you serve.'" (verse 8)

> Jesus answered him, "It is said, 'You shall not put the Lord your God to the test.'" (verse 12)

Jesus countered the lies of the devil when He quoted from the book of Deuteronomy (8:3; 6:13, 16). He rejected the lies of Satan and responded with the truth of God. Do you think there's something we're supposed to learn from this example Jesus has set for us?

Many of us have a bad habit of beating ourselves up, cata-strophizing our setbacks, and telling ourselves lies. Do any of the following sound familiar?

- "I mess everything up."
- "I'm the worst parent ever."
- "I'm a terrible spouse."
- "I'm a total failure at life."
- "My faith is so weak."
- "I'm such a hypocrite."
- "I must be the worst Christian."
- "Everyone must think poorly of me."
- "My life is totally messed up."
- "It would be easier to be dead than to keep living my miserable life."
- "Everyone hates me."
- "No one respects me."
- "I look terrible."
- "I'm not very smart."
- "I have nothing meaningful to contribute."
- "There is always someone who can accomplish just about anything better than I can."
- "My life has been a total waste."
- "I will never do anything that's truly meaningful."
- "God must be punishing me."
- "God doesn't love me, and I don't blame Him because I don't even love myself."

What would it look like if you spent the next thirty-one days replacing the lies you've believed about yourself with the truth the Lord has made clear in His Word? What would it look like if you started talking to yourself like God talks to you?

I want to challenge you to do just that. In the coming pages, we're going to begin a new conversation. We're going to dwell on the true, noble, right, pure, lovely, admirable, excellent, and praiseworthy truths God is telling us. Each day's reading begins with a truth from God's Word, followed by a narrative to give context. And while the anecdotes in the narratives are stories from my life, it is my hope that you will be able to relate to them in a way that allows you to find similar truths in your own life.

At the end of each day's reading is a "Dwell on This" challenge, which is your opportunity to change the narrative of your self-talk. You'll see that by interrupting old patterns, you can experience a dramatic transformation in the quality of your life. Are you ready to get started?

DWELL ON THESE THINGS

DAY 1

You are loved more deeply than you realize.

I have been crucified with Christ. It is no longer I who live, but Christ who lives in me. And the life I now live in the flesh I live by faith in the Son of God, who loved me and gave himself for me.

—*Galatians 2:20*

We want to be loved, but the true nature of love is often misunderstood. Many of the relationships we have in this world demonstrate a form of conditional love toward us that we have accepted as normal. Very early in life, we learn there are people who will "love" us if we either do something for them or give something to them. But if we stop doing or giving, their love disappears just as quickly as it came. So we keep doing and we keep giving, hoping to earn just a little more love. But in the end, this becomes an impossible cycle to sustain. Eventually we realize we don't have the emotional energy to continue this pattern long term.

Conditional love doesn't satisfy our hearts.

Conditional love breeds insecurity.

Conditional love isn't love at all. It's merely the utilitarian use or subtle abuse of another person, whether or not it's intended as such.

When we spend long seasons of life believing that love is conditional in nature, we eventually begin to despise others and hate ourselves. We resent the fickle ways we're treated, and we start to mistakenly believe that we may actually be unlovable.

But are you unlovable? Were you placed on this earth to be used like a commodity by other people? No. That is not God's eternal purpose for you. In fact, He makes it abundantly clear that you're loved more deeply than you realize.

When the apostle Paul wrote a letter to the churches of Galatia, he made a point to share some very personal information about himself. He wanted the events that took place in his life to demonstrate that God loves His children and displays that love in miraculous ways.

During an earlier season of Paul's life, before he came to faith in Christ and changed his name from Saul of Tarsus, he actively and intentionally persecuted Christians. He terrorized and threatened them. He helped facilitate their imprisonment and execution. But after coming to faith in Christ, he saw the wrong of his actions and declared that he wasn't the same person he once was.

I like the way Paul described his transformation: "I have been crucified with Christ. It is no longer I who live, but Christ who lives in me" (Galatians 2:20). Think about these statements for just a moment. What was Paul trying to communicate?

When Paul referred to himself as being "crucified with Christ," he was making clear that the old Paul (Saul) was dead. He wasn't the same man. His former ambitions, objectives, and goals were no longer the governing forces in his life. Jesus rescued and transformed him. Saul had died, and Paul had been reborn through faith. He was a new creation. In fact, the way Paul spoke of his new life stressed that he was now led and empowered by Jesus. Christ lived within him and would be the One directing his steps going forward.

This change in perspective was a drastic transformation in Paul's life. His entire outlook was transformed, and the hope that he now possessed was something he would ultimately give his life for in order to share that hope with others.

What motivated his transformation? I believe Paul was moved by the love of Christ. He had directly experienced unconditional love, and now he was willing to risk his life and well-being to make the love of Christ known to those who still persisted in the ignorance of unbelief.

He continued in Galatians 2:20, "The life I now live in the flesh I live by faith in the Son of God, who loved me and gave himself for me." Here Paul was telling the Galatian believers that he was convinced Jesus loved him because of the sacrifice He was willing to make on his behalf.

It's one thing to say, "I love you." It's another to demonstrate that love. Jesus displayed the depth of His love by going to the cross in our place, even while we were still living as His enemies. Paul may not have witnessed Christ's crucifixion with his own eyes, but when he wrote this letter, he could still talk to people who were at the foot of the cross. He had a clear mental image of what Christ endured on his behalf. The knowledge that Jesus would bear that torture for him amazed Paul, particularly since he knew how undeserving he was to be blessed in such a way.

During an earlier season of Paul's life, he mistakenly believed he had to earn God's love. Eventually, his heart was convinced that God's love had been demonstrated to him freely through Jesus, who died in his place. Paul was well aware of the life he'd once led and the mistakes he'd committed, but he was also awakened to the reality that he was loved in a deeper way than he'd once realized. The sacrificial death of Christ confirmed that.

Is this something you remind yourself about? Do you tell yourself you're deeply loved? Or, like Saul, do you mistakenly believe you have to earn God's love? How does what you believe about love make a difference in your life?

Years ago, when I first started offering pastoral counseling, a woman asked me if I'd be willing to meet with her and her husband. She was concerned about her marriage and wanted to seek outside help and counsel, so I agreed to meet with them. She expressed exasperation with their marriage. It seemed to her that no matter what she said, her husband wasn't interested in listening. He also struggled to verbalize what he was feeling. She conveyed that he was sensitive to anything that could be perceived as criticism, and when she tried to encourage him, he resisted her praise.

After I spoke with them both, it became clear to me that the husband had been struggling for decades with the fear that he was both unloved and unlovable. During his youth, a form of conditional love was regularly reinforced. He carried that misunderstanding of love into his marriage, and now he struggled to accept love, praise, admiration, and counsel from his wife. He misinterpreted every attempt she made to speak into his life as an attack on him.

If you could talk to that man, what would you say? What truth would you want him to embrace? How would you pray for him? What message do you think the Lord wants him to start preaching to his heart?

How do you think this man would live differently if he embraced the understanding that he was loved on a deeper level than he could possibly imagine and that his wife's affection wasn't tied to his actions? Is this a truth you've been speaking to your heart, or do you beat yourself up and drill in a message that you're unloved and unlovable? Are you mistakenly convinced that God's love is conditional, just like love you've experienced in so many other contexts of your life? Are you willing to begin believing that the absolute love of God is far superior to the false love you've been shown in your past?

It isn't a trite statement to say that Jesus loves you. He demonstrated His love for you when He graciously gave Himself for you. He endured ridicule, shame, and death on your behalf. Then He rose from death as the ultimate victor over every falsehood or principality that crushes your spirit and steals your hope.

You are loved more deeply than you realize. Allow yourself to start embracing this truth, and your heart will be refreshed.

When you have your next less-than-perfect day, remind yourself of the nature of Christ's love.

When you start believing the lie that you're unloved or unlovable, take a moment to contemplate why Christ endured the cross on your behalf. He didn't just tell you He loved you; He demonstrated it in dramatic fashion.

Over the next twenty-four hours, there are going to be all kinds of messages flashing through your mind. Some will align with the teaching of God's Word, and some will not. Confront the lies with the overwhelming truth of God's unconditional love for you.

DWELL ON THIS

Today I will remember that in Christ I am loved more deeply than I realize.

Walk by faith rather than by sight to experience greater joy.

Though you have not seen him,
you love him. Though you do not
now see him, you believe in him
and rejoice with joy that is
inexpressible and filled with glory,
obtaining the outcome of your
faith, the salvation of your souls.

—1 Peter 1:8–9

Most mornings, I drive to the gym for an hour of exercise. The gym I use has plenty of equipment, but I spend the majority of my time on a treadmill. I love it. It used to feel like a chore, but lately it's become one of my favorite activities of the day. I set the incline on the treadmill to level 11 and the pace to 2.8 miles per hour. Then I cue up a podcast, put my earbuds in, close my eyes, and walk. I spend that hour feeding my mind and heart, exercising my body, and taking a pause from walking by sight. I barely open my eyes during that hour, and I'm often surprised at how quickly the time passes.

During the rest of my waking hours, I'm primarily accustomed to watching where I'm going. I double-check for traffic before I cross streets. I heavily rely on my eyes to help me determine which direction to walk. In the physical realm, that makes sense, but from a spiritual standpoint, walking by sight is tragic.

Throughout Scripture, the Lord makes it clear that He wants us to trust Him. Faith pleases Him, and He calls us to exercise it. But it can be a very difficult transition for us to learn to walk by faith when it feels as though most contexts of life demand we walk by sight.

The apostle Peter addressed this dilemma in his first epistle. Peter was one of a select group of humans who could actually say they had seen God. During the course of His earthly ministry, Jesus Christ—God the Son—walked with Peter, taught him, challenged him, and prepared him for future service and future trials. Peter's appreciation of and love for Christ grew deeper and deeper throughout his adult life. Without a doubt, as Peter penned the words of his letter, he was looking forward to the day when he would see Jesus once again.

The majority of those who read Peter's letter, both in his generation and ours, have never seen Jesus. Even though we haven't seen Him face to face, we love Him. By the intervening power of the Holy Spirit, our spiritual eyes have been opened up to see who Jesus is and recognize our need for Him in our lives.

We need His forgiveness.

We need His righteousness.

We need His comforting presence.

Peter stressed that even though our natural eyes cannot yet view our Savior, we still believe in Him. We believe that He possesses a divine nature. We believe He has satisfied God the

Father's righteous wrath against our sin. We believe that He is sufficient to meet our every need.

The apostle Peter understood the connection between faith and joy. He wrote to the early Christians, a group of believers experiencing considerable hardship—adversities such as uncomfortable jail cells, threats, and persecution—simply because they loved and obeyed Jesus. But what did Peter remind them about through this letter? He reminded them that even though they couldn't presently see Jesus with their eyes, they could still trust Him, walk with Him by faith, and experience an inexpressible sense of joy that couldn't be diminished by their difficult circumstances. Peter encouraged them to think beyond their circumstances and dwell on the fact that the day was coming when they would receive the outcome of their faith: the salvation of their souls.

Have you ever considered just how different this belief is when compared to almost everything else? In other spheres of life, we tend to believe what we see and doubt what we cannot see. When the first snow arrives during the winter and my children look out the window and say, "It's snowing!" I want to look outside and see it for myself. When a friend tells me she liked a movie, I may consider her opinion, but I don't really know if I'm going to care for the movie until I watch it myself. When I read automotive articles that tell me about a new body design for one of my favorite car brands, I doubt whether I'll appreciate the changes until I see them with my own eyes. I'm used to walking by sight, and so are you.

But again, God delights in watching our faith mature to the point that we learn that relying on our physical vision has limited benefits. Its primary use is in the successful navigation of the natural world, but we are more than just natural beings; we are spiritual beings with physical bodies (Zechariah 12:1).

And for those who know Jesus, even our current bodies are one day going to be transformed into new, glorified ones that will no longer be subject to sin or its effects (1 Corinthians 15:44–47).

We may know that to be true, but how often do we still elect to rely primarily on natural means and physical sight to navigate the experiences, seasons, and trials of earthly life? Are you convinced that literal sight is going to bring you joy? Does your attempt to control or predict every outcome bring your heart peace, or does it feed your anxiety?

Several years ago, a college student began attending the church I pastor. He was completely blind. Physically speaking, he couldn't see a thing. One of his friends would drive him to church, but other than that ride, he would get to where he was going with the help of a Seeing Eye dog. I always enjoyed spotting his dog nestled comfortably under his seat, listening while I preached.

You know what I noticed about that student? He never seemed to be in a bad mood. He joyfully greeted me on Sunday mornings, he joyfully worshipped with the rest of our church family, and he joyfully conversed with me after worship services before heading back to campus. Now, I'm sure he had plenty of moments in life when he didn't feel so up-beat, but his demeanor reminded me of something that's taught over and over again in the Bible: true joy is not dependent on physical sight. This student's blindness made it necessary for him to learn to walk by faith in a way that many people never learn. His unmistakable contentment was a living testimony that walking by sight isn't what brings joy.

Have you ever considered that one of the reasons you may be struggling to experience joy might be that you're still convinced that seeing produces joy? Guess what? It doesn't. All it does is feed your desire to control what you can't control, predict what you can't predict, and rely on the work of your hands to sustain your sense of well-being. Walking by sight means trusting in your abilities instead of in Jesus. Doing so will eventually crush your spirit and prevent you from experiencing the blessings that come with learning to trust God in all circumstances.

Years ago, I met a man who was in a multiple-vehicle accident at high speed on his way home from work. For a time, it looked as though he wasn't going to survive, but by the grace of God, he lived. The accident was severe, though. Many of the man's bones were broken, his body was covered in lacerations, and he lost the ability to use one of his arms. His arm didn't have to be amputated, but it no longer functioned like he wanted it to. He never got over that accident. Every day, he cursed his life and often wished he were dead. His sense of identity was wrapped up in his physical abilities. In one breath, he would assure me of his strong faith in God, but in the next, he refused to believe that God had any redeeming purpose for his trial. He couldn't see that anything good could ever come from his challenge. I have rarely met someone so negative. It wasn't pleasant or edifying to spend any amount of time with that man, and eventually most people learned to avoid him.

If your whole sense of well-being is tied to what you can presently see, there's a part of you that will approach each day from the negative, unhealthy, faithless perspective of that discouraged man. You won't believe there can be a greater purpose for your trials. You'll embrace discouragement instead of rejoicing in the truth. You'll stay stuck in your momentary circumstances instead of believing that the Lord has good things in store for you. But you don't have to remain stuck in sight; you can begin to trust and learn to truly believe.

If you're currently facing a painful trial, please try to remember that it's for only a season. The Lord is in control of all things, and He can strengthen you through it and show you better things in coming days.

If you're currently worried about what is up ahead, don't fear. The Lord has already told you that the outcome of your faith is the salvation of your soul. You will see this salvation if your faith is in Christ.

If you're currently convinced that you'll experience joy only once your circumstances become more comfortable or ideal, stop lying to yourself. True joy isn't found in the momentary pleasures of this world; it is found through Jesus. And even though you haven't seen Him yet, you can see what He's doing. If you can learn to love Him more than you love the decomposing treasures of this world, He will help you see things in a brand-new way, and He will teach you to truly rejoice as your heart becomes fully convinced that He is working all things for His glory and your good.

God's desire is for you to walk by faith, assured in hope and convinced that you will one day see greater things than you could possibly conceive.

> Faith is the assurance of things hoped for, the conviction of things not seen. (Hebrews 11:1)

DWELL ON THIS

As one who has been granted a new perspective
through Christ, today I will walk by faith rather than
by sight to experience greater joy.

Let your heart be ruled by the peace of Christ.

Let the peace of Christ rule in your
hearts, to which indeed you were
called in one body. And be thankful.

—*Colossians* 3:15

Peace is an ideal that many of us value highly, but it doesn't often feel as though it's easy to obtain. Throughout my life, I have heard world leaders, prominent politicians, self-help gurus, and various salespeople promise that they could give us the peace our hearts crave. That sounds nice, but I've never seen anyone deliver on that promise.

During his era, Alexander the Great tried to find a sense of peace or contentment through conquest. As he invaded and overtook nation after nation, he rejoiced in his ability to se-cure decisive victories, but eventually even that experience left him feeling empty. It has been said that after conquering much of the known world at the time, "he wept because there were no more worlds to conquer." People debate who to at-tribute that quote to, but regardless of whether that phrase originated with Plutarch or a Hollywood script, the point is well made. Alexander was searching to experience a level of satisfaction that he believed could be obtained only through asserting his dominance over neighboring lands. He was wrong, and his heart never found the peace he sought.

The absence of peace is something we feel in a profound way. It influences the quality of our day and our outlook toward the future. It can affect what our minds dwell on and even hold us back from doing what the Lord has designed us to do.

For me, finding peace at nighttime is hard. I never have been a great sleeper. I'm envious of my wife and my youngest son, who both have the ability to fall asleep, on cue, every night at ten thirty. It fascinates me. It's as if their internal clocks nudge them at that very minute each evening and tell them to close their eyes and fall asleep.

I, on the other hand, get a burst of energy each evening right around the time they're calling it a night. In fact, a high percentage of my books and blog posts are composed when most people are sleeping.

Several years ago, I went through a prolonged stretch of staying awake much later than even I usually do. I would go to bed at a reasonable time (for me), but when my head hit the pillow, I could not fall asleep. For hours, I would glance frequently at my alarm clock, and as each hour ticked by, I would become progressively more irritated that I was still awake.

During those hours, my mind would swim with activity. I would think about all sorts of tasks I still needed to accomplish. I would worry about the health of the church I serve. I would envision every what-if scenario possible about calamities that could potentially happen to my family. It was unpleasant, and it persisted for quite a while.

I tried a few things to correct the problem. I started drinking decaf coffee. It didn't work. I stopped checking my cell phone once I went to bed. That helped a little, but not enough. I listened to biographical and historical podcasts at night, and that helped a lot, but it wasn't the cure. I even took a two-day retreat to a cabin in a different part of the state. That was refreshing, but it wasn't the ultimate solution.

The vital fix came when I realized that my issue wasn't biological or circumstantial; my issue was spiritual. I was trying to control what only God has control over. I was trying to predict things only God knows. And the Lord began showing me areas of sin in my heart that I needed to repent of. My lack of sleep and the absence of peace in my life were very much connected to the fact that I was compartmentalizing the Lord while also trying my best to call the shots in my life instead of trusting Him to do so.

In Colossians 3:15, Paul spoke of true and lasting peace. He referenced the kind of peace our hearts truly crave, but we often mistakenly believe that peace can be obtained from faulty or ineffective sources. The peace we crave—and need—can be found only in Jesus. This is a truth we need to tell ourselves often. This is a truth that our controlling, sinful, worldly perspectives will regularly fight against, to our own detriment. Our desire to rule what isn't under our control leaves us feeling empty and defeated. It exposes an emotional and spiritual void.

Voids don't tend to stay vacant for long. You've probably noticed that in most groups or organizations, leadership voids tend to be filled rather quickly. This happens in governments, families, and even the local church. A coveted position doesn't remain open forever. Eventually, a dominant personality will emerge and attempt to fill it because the desire to rule is a powerful impulse that we resist handing over to others, even those we claim to trust.

God's Word encourages us to let the peace of Christ rule in our hearts. The rule of Christ is benevolent, and His leadership can be trusted without question. Ironically, although we certainly enjoy peace, we struggle to allow ourselves to be "ruled," even by Jesus. By nature, we want to be in charge of our lives. We want to be the boss. We want to hold the reins of control. But our desire for control fights against our yearning for peace. As long as we insist on remaining in control, we won't experience the peace we crave.

As followers of Jesus who possess deep and abiding trust in Him, we're called to let His peace rule in our lives. His peace should govern our hearts. His peace should be the expression of His nature, which overshadows our emotions and cognition. We need to stop deceiving ourselves into believing that our hearts will find the rest we seek anywhere else. I think this is something Paul was trying to help us understand when he penned Colossians 3:15.

As believers in Christ, we have been called, in one body, to experience His peace together. I don't know about you, but there are plenty of people in this world, including some of my brothers and sisters in Christ, whom I struggle to get along with at times. Whether it was differing preferences or priorities, or personalities that rubbed me the wrong way, there have been relationships in which harmony felt unattainable.

Yet we are called as His family to live in peace with one another. When our hearts are being ruled by the peace of Christ, the outpouring of that reality will be the intentional fostering of unity, compassion, and trust among believers.

Additionally, as Paul stressed, we'll be divinely empowered to be thankful. A peaceful heart is a thankful heart. It exudes gratitude and can operate from a place of contentment because a peaceful heart knows that Christ already has provided all it needs and will continue to do so.

While this is the kind of lesson I'll be learning throughout my life, I'm grateful for what the Lord has enabled me to grasp so far. As I'm learning to welcome the rule of Christ's peace in my heart, I'm sleeping better. I'm still a "late bird" in many respects, but when my head hits the pillow, I entrust my desire for control, my cares, and my worries to Him. The more I actually do this, the more I learn to value the peace Christ offers me.

Is this your story too, or are you still telling yourself that you need to be the boss who calls the shots? Are you trying to control what you can't control? Are you letting your mind be dominated by what-if scenarios? Are you being robbed of sleep because your heart isn't at rest?

You will never find peace if you're trying to rule.

You will never be at rest if you're convinced you need to do God's job for Him.

But let's be honest. In one breath, it's easy for us to acknowledge our need for the peace of Christ to rule over our hearts, but in the other breath, we try to proclaim our own independence and desire for spiritual self-rule. Like Alexander discovered centuries ago, feeding our desires for conquest will never produce the inner peace we crave.

When the peace of Christ rules in our hearts, we'll be content to trust the Lord's direction and instruction.

When the peace of Christ rules in our hearts, we'll demonstrate the kind of humility that invites Him to lead and guide.

When the peace of Christ rules in our hearts, we'll be able to go through life in a state of contented appreciation for the work He has already accomplished on our behalf. He makes us capable of and comfortable with living in a kingdom we did not build.

If the desire to obtain spiritual self-rule has been your pattern, you may need to come to a crisis point before this changes. The Lord may need to break you of your desire to war against His peace. One of the greatest blessings He might allow to come into your life is a crisis that brings you to your knees and forces you to admit that you don't have the strength or wisdom necessary to carry your burdens without Him. In that moment, you can continue to try to fight against Jesus or you can embrace the opportunity He's giving you to submit your heart over to Him.

Peace is not found within yourself. You will find peace only at the source: Jesus. Peace will come when you welcome Him to reign in your life as the Lord of your heart.

DWELL ON THIS

Today I will let my heart be ruled by the peace of Christ and give up my desire for spiritual self-rule.

Any trial can be an occasion for joy.

Count it all joy, my brothers, when
you meet trials of various kinds, for
you know that the testing of your
faith produces steadfastness.

—*James* 1:2–3

Trials come in all shapes and sizes. Some of our trials occupy only a single day or a brief moment; others can drag on for longer seasons, sometimes even years. We may find ourselves spending a considerable amount of emotional energy counting the days until the trial is over. But wishing away our time is not the best way to spend our lives.

It's easy to fall into the false expectation that as followers of Christ we are going to be free of pain, grief, opposition, and confusion. When God allows trials to come into our lives, we question His wisdom and assume He's making mistakes or ignoring our plights. But trials and adversity are inevitable parts of life. The Lord uses these experiences to deepen our faith and strengthen our reliance on Him. Some of our greatest long-term blessings are the fruit of our short-term trials.

Knowing this helps us make better sense of James 1:2–3.

James, an early-church leader, understood the weight of adversity. In his brief letter, he makes many interesting statements that effectively confront our shortsighted expectations. When it comes to our trials, James advises us to consider them occasions for joy. I wonder how many people have laughed at or even bristled against James's teaching when they first read his counsel. When reading what James wrote, you may have thought:

- *How am I supposed to be joyful in the midst of a family crisis?*
- *I don't see any joy in the loss of my job and the destabilization of our household income.*
- *If James understood the level of conflict I'm having at home, he would have given me different advice.*
- *Watching my mother die from disease doesn't strike me as an occasion for joy.*

James wasn't trying to negate the emotional experiences trials bring. Instead, he wanted us to see beyond the momentary pain of our trials into the glorious and beneficial outcome the Lord has in store for those who trust Him.

Consider some of the most valuable lessons you've learned during the course of your life. How did you learn those things? In many instances, the best lessons came from challenging or painful experiences. And while I'm sure you wouldn't want to relive those moments, let's acknowledge the wisdom and empathy you gained through your pain.

I understand the difficulty in appreciating trials. I'm an oldest child and I have two younger sisters, and the experience we had while growing up was quite challenging. Our parents are both wonderful people who have made immense investments in our lives, but their marriage exploded when my siblings and I were very young. During that season, we were surrounded by a lot of conflict, and our patterns, routines, and living arrangements changed dramatically, almost in an instant.

My parents, amid the challenging waters of raising children together while being at odds with one another, had to sell our home. In desperation, we were forced to move into government housing, which after a few years was followed by moving into a house that should have been condemned.

Finances became so tight and our life so disorganized that there were extended periods when we didn't have heat or running water. While our parents tried to sort out our changing family dynamics, my sisters and I felt shuffled around and in the way. We were dealing with a whole host of problems that were the result of others' decisions. There wasn't much we could do about the issues we were experiencing other than pray, cope, learn, and adapt.

During that season of life, especially into my teen years, I started to feel emotionally overwhelmed and exasperated with the chaos. To give myself a respite from the confusion, I did my best to avoid being home. As soon as I was old enough to drive, I bought a well-used Oldsmobile Cutlass Ciera for eight hundred dollars at an auto auction. As long as it had gas in the tank, it could take me far away from family conflict. I also made a point to work before and after school, on weekends, and all summer in order to stay busy and distant. And when I could fit it in with my work schedule, I played a few sports. I came home to sleep, but I usually tried to be anywhere else. I'm grateful that eventually things began to improve with our family, but that didn't really start to take hold until I was in college.

When I went to college, I arrived there with the goal of preparing to become a high school history teacher. I knew I liked to teach, and I thought I might enjoy helping students develop an appreciation for various leaders and cultures that have shaped historical eras. But God had a different plan for my life, which He started to make clear to me during my sophomore year. Through several key experiences and the counsel of friends and mentors, the Lord impressed upon my heart the desire to become a pastor. I had been resisting that calling out of fear, but I couldn't resist it any longer. When I finally made peace with what God was asking, I took the necessary courses and training to prepare me to serve in that role of church leadership. Within three weeks of finishing college, at the tender age of twenty-one, I was standing behind the pulpit of my first church.

As I reflect on my past through the lens of time, I am able to better see what God was up to. It's clear to me now that He used the trials of my youth to prepare me for my future role and responsibilities. When my parents' marriage ended, God taught me that I can rely on Him to meet my needs and provide stability in my life. When confronted with problems born out of someone else's decisions, I learned the importance of walking by faith and holding on to hope. He taught me not to catastrophize my momentary trials. He taught me about self-discipline. Through the care I provided for my younger siblings, He also taught me what it's like to lead others and look out for their needs.

There were many aspects of my childhood that I disliked, but I wouldn't go back and change any of it now, even if I could. The Lord used those hard, chaotic days to deepen my reliance on Him. He taught me how to navigate difficult seasons and prepared me for the responsibilities I now have. Although my college classes were certainly helpful and practical, they couldn't compare to the lessons I learned by walking with the Lord in the valleys. By His grace, I quickly matured and was able to serve in a leadership role at a very young age, largely because of the growth I experienced through the painful trials of my youth.

If you're going through a hard time right now, don't let it become a cause for despair. Yes, trials can be miserable. Yes, they're painful. Yes, you probably wish they were over already. But I promise you that God won't waste what He's presently allowing you to endure. Given time and a dose of hindsight, you'll begin to see the reasons from a higher vantage point. Something good will come from it all.

I realize that might sound crazy, particularly if your current trial is intense, but James wasn't speaking as someone who lived a cushy, uneventful, trial-free life. He experienced pain, grief, and the confusion that can come from exceedingly arduous situations.

During his early years, James experienced ridicule. He was the half brother of Jesus, but even he didn't grow up believing in Jesus's divinity. In fact, James didn't come to faith in Christ until after Jesus's resurrection. During his formative years, James endured the critical focus on their family as people either marveled at Jesus or mocked Him. I imagine that in the years before James came to faith in Christ, he found the attention he received because of his association with Jesus grating and upsetting.

James endured the shame of his brother being arrested and then executed as a criminal, compounding his trials. He also experienced the grief of his mother, Mary, at Jesus's torture and death.

Then, after Christ's resurrection, James came to believe in Jesus as the Son of God. He went from disbelief to faith, and people he had called friends and brothers in his former religious tradition now considered him a traitor. No matter which side he chose, he was going to disappoint someone.

Yet James endured. He knew the Lord would bring goodness from these trials, so he persisted and became devout in his prayer life. It's rumored that the amount of time he spent on his knees before the Lord in worship would eventually cause his knees to become knobby and calloused, like those of a camel.* But the Lord blessed him with wisdom. He became a prominent, respected elder. He grew to become someone the early church honored and sought counsel from.

James was eventually martyred. He refused to deny his faith in Christ and was thrown to the ground from the roof of the temple in Jerusalem. While on the ground, he was subsequently beaten with a club until he died. As horrendous as that was, James knew to look beyond the momentary pain and fix his eyes on the glory the Lord had in store for him. His joy was in Christ, not in a comfortable, earthly experience.

When James spoke of trials, he didn't speak as someone who was unfamiliar with them. He knew what genuine trials were, and he understood that trials don't need to dictate emotions. When viewed through the benevolent and sovereign eyes of the Lord, our trials can be seen as occasions for joy. Joy is not happiness. Happiness is dependent on circumstances, while joy is not. True joy is an abiding confidence in Jesus and the assurance that He truly is working all circumstances together for our good.

---

* John Pollock, *The Apostle: A Life of Paul* (Colorado Springs, CO: David C Cook, 2012), 114.

Is your life marked by the joy of the Lord?

What are you preaching to your heart as you endure your present pain?

Do you believe the Lord is working all things together for your good?

It's time to tell yourself that real joy is anchored in the nature of God, not in the transient nature of your circumstances.

DWELL ON THIS

> Though my momentary pain may be excruciating, any trial I encounter today can be an occasion for joy.

Dwell on God's kindness toward you.

God, being rich in mercy, because
of the great love with which he
loved us, even when we were dead
in our trespasses, made us alive
together with Christ—by grace you
have been saved—and raised us up
with him and seated us with him
in the heavenly places in Christ
Jesus, so that in the coming ages he
might show the immeasurable
riches of his grace in kindness
toward us in Christ Jesus.

—*Ephesians 2:4–7*

What would you do if you were asked to save a life and it was
in your power to do so? Would you seize the opportunity, or
would you run in fear from such a weighty responsibility?
What if instead of one life you were asked to save the lives of
nine million people? Would you do it?

More than a century ago, there was a man who attempted
such a task—and succeeded.

If you're familiar with American presidential history, you probably know the name Herbert Hoover. Hoover served as president for one term that began in the late 1920s. To this day, many people know him only as the president who served in office when the stock market crashed and the Great Depression began. That's tragic because there's much more to Hoover than that. In fact, I would contend that the more significant events of his life took place before his presidency.

Hoover studied engineering and became a prosperous entrepreneur at a young age. A large percentage of his wealth was acquired through mining, but he wanted to use his life for more than accumulating riches. Hoover was a kind and compassionate man, and deep within his heart he had a desire to help others in meaningful ways. He wanted to make a difference with his life. He wanted to make the lives of other people better, and during World War I, he was given a significant opportunity to do so.

Early in the days of the war, Germany invaded Belgium. Within three months, the people of Belgium were close to running out of food. If their food ran out, millions of people would most certainly starve to death. The thought of mass starvation occurring in this neutral country was unthinkable to many world leaders, so a plan was devised that would enable food to be safely delivered to them without further entanglement with any of the warring parties. Hoover, who had already established himself as a great humanitarian and organizer, was asked to oversee this important mission.

Hoover didn't need to do this. He was already a wealthy man and didn't need to use his talents to aid a foreign nation, but he felt compelled to do so. With great generosity and kindness, he gave himself completely to this effort to save the Belgians from starvation. He ensured that food was distributed to every needy area of the country. Famine was averted, and over the next few years, nine million people were fed.* As people around the world watched Hoover orchestrate and administer this great relief effort, he was given a nickname. He was frequently called the Great Humanitarian, but few people are aware of that now. It's amazing how quickly we can forget acts of great kindness.

Hoover was an optimist and looked for ways he could show kindness to others. In general, I would consider myself an optimistic person as well, particularly when it comes to observing God's hand at work. I'm convinced that everything is going to work out the way God intended. I believe the Lord has a plan that will come to fruition with intentionality, and I'm looking forward to the blessings and everlasting provisions He has in store for millions and millions of His children. I believe this, yet my mind doesn't always dwell on the depths of His kindness.

Instead, I am too frequently swept up with the issues and concerns of the day. I fret about matters outside my control. And in those moments, I sometimes forget to look for God's kindness.

My wife, Andrea, doesn't seem to overlook God's kindness like I do. When we're praying together, particularly after faith-stretching moments, she thanks God for His kindness toward us. This aspect of His character catches her attention. I would even go so far as to say that it may be what she appreciates most about Him.

Ephesians 2:7 reminds us that God is kind and delights to show His kindness to His children through "the immeasur-

---

* Encyclopedia Britannica online, s.v. "Herbert Hoover," www.britannica .com/biography/Herbert-Hoover.

able riches of his grace." God wants us to see and experience riches of grace, a treasure that surpasses the glory of the earthly riches our hearts are prone to admire.

I'm grateful for what this verse reveals about the heart of God because it stands in contrast with the priorities that often grip the hearts of humanity. I'm reminded of a time when I was in high school and my mother's job was to provide home health care. One afternoon, she brought me along to visit one of her clients. He was a wealthy man who owned an impressive property. His mobility was limited and he couldn't speak clearly, but he insisted on giving us a tour of his estate via a golf cart. We politely sat on the back of the cart and took the tour. He pointed out the land he owned, his opulent house, the bird sanctuary behind his home, and a Rolls-Royce in his garage. I attempted to act impressed, but I had never heard of the carmaker, nor did I realize how expensive the automobiles were. Here was a man who had the finest things this world offered, and his sense of self-worth was tied up in showing those things off.

But, unlike this rich man, God isn't interested in showing off the immeasurable riches of His grace; rather, He wants to share them with us. He desires to bless His children with an inheritance that holds more value than any human estate. That's what He has in store for us. That's something we should be thinking about in our quiet moments and daydreams.

God is kind, generous, and giving.

He's kind when He answers our prayers.

He's kind when He gives us the exact opposite of what we requested because He knows what we really need.

He's kind when He warms our hearts by reassuring us of His presence.

He's kind when He breaks our hearts in order to bring us back to the place where we realize He is all we've ever needed.

It doesn't stop there, though. In Ephesians 2:7, Paul reminds us that the kindness of God is shown *toward us*. It isn't just displayed in front of us or behind us; it is directed at us. Our well-being matters to our Creator. He's operating in our best interests.

It's vital for us to understand that the grace we're being shown is in *Christ Jesus*. The work He accomplished on our behalf and the future glory He holds in store for us are kindnesses that should never be far from our minds. When Christ came to this earth, He did so in order to accomplish things none of us could do. He lived sinlessly because we were enslaved to sin. He took our condemnation upon Himself at the cross because He didn't want us to remain under the wrath of God. He assured us in His resurrection that there is life after physical death for those who know Him and are united with Him.

Jesus was willing to endure the ultimate sacrifice in order to set us free from our bondage to sin, grant us new life, and secure a permanent place for us in His kingdom. When we choose to focus on the realities of this truth, our hearts and lips overflow with gratitude and praise to God.

There may be days when instead of dwelling on the kindness of God, you begin to dwell on lesser things, such as

- your own shortcomings, both real and imagined
- the pain others have caused you
- your regrets
- the judgment you feel you deserve or the judgment you fear is still in store

Just as the people of Belgium were starving for food, our hearts are often starving for reminders of God's kindness and generosity. Knowing that to be so, the Holy Spirit inspired Paul to pen a reminder to shift our minds toward thinking about the praiseworthy kindness we've been shown in Christ:

> Whatever is true, whatever is honorable, whatever is just, whatever is pure, whatever is lovely, whatever is commendable, if there is any excellence, if there is anything worthy of praise, think about these things. (Philippians 4:8)

As the Holy Spirit influences us and transforms our thinking, we begin to see things as they really are. The fog lifts; our minds begin to dwell on things that are true, honorable, just, pure, lovely, commendable, excellent, and worthy of praise; and our inner monologue shifts to reveal God's kindness toward us.

Our God is more than a great humanitarian; He's our creator, father, and friend. He never misses a chance to show His kindness to those He loves.

DWELL ON THIS

> Today I will dwell on God's kindness toward me and thank Him for sharing the riches of His grace with me.

DAY 6

Give grace to those around you.

I therefore, a prisoner for the Lord,
urge you to walk in a manner
worthy of the calling to which you
have been called, with all humility
and gentleness, with patience,
bearing with one another in love,
eager to maintain the unity of the
Spirit in the bond of peace.

—*Ephesians 4:1–3*

Few things in life have stretched me as much as having children. I love my kids and thoroughly enjoy spending time with them, but they don't do everything the same way I do or the way I like it done. And it's not because they're all jerks. In fact, of the four, I would say that less than 50 percent of them are jerks at a given time (but at the time of this writing, all four are teenagers, so draw your own conclusions of my current emotional state).

When my wife and I got married, we had to learn the strategic dance of honoring each other's preferences. Within eleven seconds of getting that figured out, we started having children. Over the span of five and a half years, four kids showed up. And surprisingly, they're all different from one another. It amazes me how four kids growing up in the same exact environment with the same parents can be so different. But they are.

One child is relatively quiet and likes studying foreign languages. Another child is strong willed and hates being photographed. Another is deferential toward others but cannot be woken up after falling asleep on the couch. Another makes friends with everyone but refuses to laugh at my jokes.

If my kids bother to read this chapter someday, they need to know it bugs me when they leave crumbs on the counter in front of the toaster, block the front door with their shoes, or have more clothing on their bedroom floors than in their closets. But even though I crab about these things (like most parents do), I also realize that life isn't about getting everything I prefer 100 percent of the time. It has been healthy for me to be forced to put up with the growing pains of living with infants who became toddlers, and then became middle schoolers, and then became teenagers, and are now on the cusp of becoming adults. And I have it easy compared to the adults who had to put up with me when I was going through those stages of development. As an adult, I have felt compelled to apologize to many of them.

The reality of our situation is that we all have our weaknesses. We all have areas in which we haven't fully matured. Whether we know it or not, we're all trying someone's patience. It doesn't make sense for me to withhold patience toward others when I need theirs to be shown to me so regularly. But through Christ, we're empowered to bear with the weaknesses, preferences, and maturity level of others.

The early church wasn't immune to this phenomenon. An

interesting group of people from different backgrounds and ethnicities were united together into one body through their common faith in Christ. But as you can imagine, the process of learning to deal with each other's differences wasn't always easy.

When apostles, evangelists, and elders attempted to reach new people groups with the gospel and then shepherd those who responded, they had quite the task. At times, it was likely frustrating and maybe even intimidating. Most people, even Christians, can take a somewhat threatening posture when their preferences are being challenged.

For that reason, Scripture encourages us to walk in a manner that's worthy of our calling. We've been called into relationship with Christ. We've been granted new lives and new ways of thinking. We've been united together as one family with all who believe, and we've been empowered to become fully devoted followers of Christ together.

If we're walking in a manner that's worthy of that calling, we're going to model the mindset of Christ toward others. We're going to attempt to bear with the weaknesses of our comrades. We're going to try to see preferences and circumstances through their eyes.

The Bible encourages us to do so with humility and gentleness, not arrogance and harshness. Instead of puffing ourselves up and treating our brothers and sisters abrasively, we are to respond gently toward those who may not see things the way we see them or haven't reached the level of social or spiritual maturity we're presently enjoying.

In practical terms, this admonishment reminds me of an incident that my wife told me about recently when she and I met for lunch at a great Thai restaurant near her office at a local university. I asked her how her day was going and if anything of note was taking place on campus. She explained that an unknown colleague (who hasn't confessed yet) broke the copier for the second time in two weeks. Both times, this person had tried to run address labels through the machine, and in each case, those labels stuck to an internal roller. The copier made loud screeching noises, and subsequent copies came out distorted.

The repairman returned to fix the copier again, and just after he began his work, one of the professors sent a document to the copier to print. It wasn't until the professor walked out of her office that she saw that the copier was in the process of being repaired. She apologized to the repairman for not knowing the machine wasn't working, but he didn't reply. Then when my wife stepped out of her office and politely greeted the man, he only made a small, monosyllabic grunting noise. I'm guessing that his patience with their copier problems had been stretched. As a result, his response to their courtesy was dismissive, abrasive, and hurtful.

This makes me wonder how often I have reflected that man's reaction instead of the heart of Christ when I'm responding to frustrating situations. Have I hurt others by reacting out of impatience and annoyance? Have I become so focused on my own issues and tasks that I have failed to show concern for how my words and body language might be causing someone else to feel dismissed and devalued?

Scripture encourages us to be patient with one another, giving each other time to grow and enough space to mature. So, are we being patient, or are we demanding immediate maturity and perfection from those we're called to love?

Bearing with one another in love isn't the easiest of tasks. To genuinely love others involves seeking what is best for them, even at great personal cost to ourselves. I'd like to say that I always remember to do that, but actually I only *sometimes* remember. In fact, sometimes I bear with others more from a sense of duty than of love.

The Bible calls on us to reflect the love of Christ. Jesus said, "Your love for one another will prove to the world that you are my disciples" (John 13:35, NLT). Consider what that means, which is that the love we show one another will give the most credence to the faith we profess. That's what an unbelieving world will find compelling. That's what a hard heart will find refreshing. That's what a lost soul will find stirring.

As love pervades the culture of the church, a genuine sense of peace will prevail in our relationships, and we'll be visibly reminded that the Holy Spirit has bonded us together as one. The world needs to see this, and so do we.

Sometime today, someone is going to test your patience. Someone is going to insult your intelligence, inconvenience you, make you feel unappreciated, or prove to you that he values his own preferences over yours.

Sometime this week, you're going to interact with someone who has a history of getting on your nerves. You're going to be tempted to avoid her or cut off your conversation with her abruptly.

Sometime this month, you're going to meet people you've never met. They aren't going to give you a good impression of themselves. You'll be glad you don't have to interact with them regularly. You may even tell yourself that you're glad you may never see them again.

Sometime this year, you're going to get together with your extended family. They do things you don't do, hold opinions you're opposed to, and make decisions you're certain are going to lead to unintended and unfortunate consequences.

This Sunday, you're going to sit near people in your church

that you're friends with only because of your connection with
Christ. You'll be tempted to greet them half-heartedly.

Love them all.

Pray for them.

Don't avoid them.

In love, with great patience, Jesus bears with your weaknesses. Through the Holy Spirit, your faith has been nour-
ished and your spiritual walk is maturing. Knowing that your
Lord is continuing to work on you, be patient with others
who are also works in progress and at earlier stages of growth.

Tell yourself that you can bear with the weaknesses, preferences, and maturity level of others.

DWELL ON THIS

> Today I will give grace to those around me because
> grace has been generously lavished on me.

You can rely on God's unconditional love.

We have come to know and to
believe the love that God has for us.
God is love, and whoever abides in
love abides in God, and God abides
in him.

—1 John 4:16

It is a wonderful privilege to raise children, but it can also involve plenty of heartbreak, particularly when you witness your kids experiencing the pain of being let down or betrayed by their friends.

I'm sure there are people in this world who think of the middle school years as wonderful, but from my own experiences and what I have observed in the lives of my children, those years can be very difficult. Your body and mind start going through drastic changes. Your emotions feel as though they're all over the place. Your peers can be cruel. It's a season that many of us would rather not repeat.

My youngest daughter is in middle school. She's the last of our four kids to have to run through that gauntlet of challenges. If you met my daughter, you would quickly realize several things about her: She knows how to get along with people her own age and people who are older than her. She endears herself to people easily. Her faith in Christ matters to her, and she makes a point to show Christlike love to others.

I think everyone should love her in return, but unfortunately that isn't the case.

Recently, she was invited to a party at a friend's house. It was just a small group of middle schoolers who were going to get some pizza, play games, and hang out for a few hours. We gave her permission to go, and she was looking forward to it. On the afternoon of the party, the friend who was hosting it decided to disinvite her without explanation. When my wife told me, my heart sank for my daughter. We all know the painful feeling of being excluded.

When I got home that evening, my daughter was alone in her room. I invited her to come down to the kitchen so we could talk. I told her I knew what had happened and that I completely understood she might be feeling down and disappointed but that I wanted her to listen carefully as I shared four undeniable truths with her. Here's what I said:

- "What your friend did to you was wrong, but it was also a favor in disguise. She let you know that your friendship wasn't genuine and that you'd be better off investing your time in your real friends."
- "You are loved more deeply than you realize. I love you, your mother loves you, and, most importantly, the Lord loves you. Our love for you is not conditional. We will never stop loving you."
- "Remember that your identity is in Christ, not in the opinions of your peers. If someone disrespects you or has a poor opinion of you, you don't need to

adopt that person's opinion as your own, because
you already know who you are in Jesus."
- "You don't need to add anything to the drama of
what took place by texting your friends about it or
changing your demeanor toward those who
offended you. Just continue to be you. Don't let this
drag you down. Make a point to be kind, even to
those who weren't kind to you."

After we were done speaking, my daughter told me that it
was helpful for her to hear those words. Overall, she had been
handling this disappointment well, even before we spoke. But
hearing those truths spoken aloud and openly was reassuring
to her heart.

I'm grateful we can rely on the love the Lord has for us. I'm
grateful His love isn't temperamental. I'm grateful that
through the counsel of His Word, the internal witness of the
Holy Spirit, and the observations we can make about how He
is working in our lives, we can both know and believe the love
God has for us. That's something the apostle John tried to
make clear in his brief letter to believers in the Bible.

John made a point to tell us that God is love. I think that's
an interesting statement that's worth thinking about. In making that statement, John went beyond asserting that God
shows us love. It's true that God shows us love and is loving
toward us, but there's a reason He is able to do so perfectly.

John revealed to us in this passage that, by nature, God is
love. When He expresses love toward us, He's doing so as an
extension or application of who He is. When God shows us
perfect love, He's taking that action because, by nature, He is
perfect love. And since He is the perfection of love, we can
rely on the love He bestows upon us.

Perfect love doesn't fail.

Perfect love isn't fussy.

Perfect love doesn't disinvite us.

Perfect love doesn't abandon us.

I was reminded of that last point recently. I sat down on a Sunday afternoon to eat a sandwich and watch the Philadelphia Eagles play the Chicago Bears. I had just come home from a busy morning at church and knew I had to be back at the church in a few hours for the activities of that evening, but I blocked off some time that afternoon to sit in my recliner, eat a nice lunch, relax, and watch the game.

Then I got a text. It said, "If the Eagles win, we are no longer friends."

It was from a friend of mine who is also a pastor. He grew up in the South but adopted the Bears as his team when he met and married his wife (whose family members are diehard Bears fans). He still resents the fact that the Eagles knocked the Bears out of the playoffs not long ago after tipping a field-goal attempt and causing the ball to hit the post.

I replied, "I'm a pastor. I'm used to conditional friendships."

He got a big kick out of that because he could relate. Of course I said that in jest, though sometimes humor can be a coping mechanism for me. I have been reflecting recently on the conditional nature of many of the relationships in my life.

In my ministry role, there are people who genuinely love me, but there are others who pretend to love me so they can use me to further their agendas. I've become pretty good at sniffing that out, and to some degree, I've grown used to it. But it's definitely not my favorite aspect of serving in this role. In an ideal world, I'd experience more unconditional love, but I realize that our sin natures tend to get in the way of that. I'm conscious of the ways I've been shown conditional love and conditional friendship, and I'm sure there are people who would say that's also what they've received from me.

That's why I'm grateful that God's love and the ways in which He shows it are perfect. He isn't my friend one moment and then my adversary the next. He doesn't love me for a year and then demonize me for a decade. He loves me, abides in me, and empowers me to remain in His love forever. That's what 1 John 4:16 reveals, and that's something I need to remind myself regularly.

Is that something you tell yourself? Are you convinced that you can rely on God's love?

The love of God doesn't mirror the flaky nature of our earthly relationships. His love can be counted on. His love isn't temperamental. His love remains the same for us on our best days and on our worst ones.

How can I be so certain that God's love for us remains constant even when we're at our lowest point? Consider what Jesus said in John 6:37: "All that the Father gives me will come to me, and whoever comes to me I will never cast out."

In this verse, Jesus made it perfectly clear that He will never cast out anyone who comes to Him with genuine faith. But is that a message we're preaching to our hearts on a daily basis? Is that a message we're conveying to our children? Is that a truth we're allowing ourselves to rest in when it feels as though we've been unfairly disinvited to the party everyone else is attending?

When you wake up each morning, you have no idea what your day is going to bring. You may have your schedule all planned out and your agenda set, but before you know it, un-invited drama can work its way in and completely alter your plans. After a particularly dramatic day recently, I commented to my wife, "I'm glad I didn't know what today was going to look like before I got out of bed this morning. If I knew, I'm not so sure I would have gotten up."

But here's the thing: God's love can be relied on when you're in the middle of drama. God's love can be relied on when your friends desert you. God's love can be relied on when you've made major mistakes. God's love can be relied on when you're trying to bounce back from whatever's got you down.

God delights in abiding in His people. He delights in showing His children grace and mercy when the rest of the world is trying to crush us. He won't run from you when you're in the midst of your low moments. Your day will be different if it begins and ends with you telling yourself these things.

DWELL ON THIS

Though people with whom I have conditional relationships may disinvite and abandon me, I can rely on God's unconditional love today and every day.

Cast your anxiety on God instead of bearing the weight yourself.

Humble yourselves, therefore,
under the mighty hand of God so
that at the proper time he may
exalt you, casting all your anxieties
on him, because he cares for you.

—1 Peter 5:6–7

I'm in a season of life and ministry that requires me to have an unusually high amount of responsibility on my plate. My wife and I are still caring for our teenage children, but we're also starting to assist our parents more and more. For five years while her health was failing, my mother lived with us part time and with my sister part time. My sibling and I shared the responsibility of caring for her until she passed away.

In addition to having family responsibilities, I'm also the lead pastor of our church. Most issues or needs in our congregation come across my desk, as I'm the primary leader and teacher. I think many people would be surprised to know how many calls, texts, emails, or drop-in visits their pastor handles on a daily basis. That's not a complaint; it's just the reality of being in this role. I also walk with people through some of the most difficult seasons of their lives. The emotional burden of my job can sometimes feel quite heavy.

Additionally, several years ago, I became the director of a mission board that helps support struggling churches, plant new ones, and encourage pastors and their families. I'm currently working closely with seven churches to help them select new pastoral leadership and develop revitalization plans. On top of that, I'm coaching and training five church planters who are at various stages of planting new churches.

As if that weren't enough, two weeks ago, I was asked to help mediate a major conflict in a church. Then I received a call yesterday that a pastor had abruptly resigned. A few hours later, someone else called asking for help investigating an accusation brought against a member of their church. While this was taking place, I was also trying to be a good husband to my wife by picking out a new couch and taking her to a movie. It was a stressful day in the middle of a busy life.

More and more, I can relate to the sentiment Paul expressed when he said, "Apart from other things, there is the daily pressure on me of my anxiety for all the churches" (2 Corinthians 11:28). I understand what it's like to deal with trials or attempt to accomplish daily tasks with that kind of pressure lingering in the back of my mind.

But here's what I've learned about anxiety and worry: It's more destructive when it's allowed to operate in secret. It's more damaging when we try to carry those emotions without help. I'm grateful that I'm surrounded by a strong team of leaders and volunteers in my church and other ministries who help me carry the burdens of ministry. I don't want to think about what it would be like to serve in this role without their support. I'm also particularly grateful for my wife, who offers a listening ear when I need to talk and tangible help with every ministry I have ever been called to serve. She is a gift from God and a visible reminder of His grace to me. Because I have a true partner in her, I have never felt alone in ministry.

The Lord has not designed you to carry your burdens alone. If you've been experiencing anxiety in recent days, could it be you're trying to do too much without the help you need? Could it be you're trying to carry a burden by yourself that you weren't designed to carry alone? Is it possible you've forgotten the counsel of Scripture telling you to cast your burdens on the Lord?

In 1 Peter 5:7, Peter counseled believers experiencing seasons of need and peril to cast their anxieties on God. They were encouraged to give their worries and cares over to the Lord. They were challenged, once and for all, to stop burdening their minds and hearts with fear, anxious thoughts, and what-if scenarios that they weren't designed to bear.

God is sovereign. He is in complete control. He can see what lies ahead and knows how everything is going to work out. This is true on the grand scale, and it's true in your individual life. God knows the trials you will face and which struggles He is going to divinely prevent you from experiencing. You are His child, so everything He allows you to endure will be for your long-term benefit, even if that involves short-term pain.

I think sometimes we allow anxiety to get the best of us because we stop telling ourselves that God is good. We forget about His kindness. We forget about His compassion. We buy into the mindset that portrays God as solely angry and vengeful. But that is not the truth God speaks to us. First Peter 5:7, the same verse that tells us to cast our anxiety on God, reveals that He "cares for you."

God cares for me? God cares for me? I often forget to tell myself that. I grow so used to His blessings that I neglect to give His goodness a second thought. Do you do the same? What would it mean for you to pause and reflect on the various ways He cares for you? Here are some truths to consider:

God cares for your material needs. You may not have every physical resource you crave, the largest house, or the fattest bank account, but you have what you need for today. Has the Lord provided air for you to breathe? Sunlight to warm your body? Food and water for you to consume? Shelter to protect you from wind and rain?

God cares for your spiritual longings. He designed you to be in relationship with Him. Back in the days of Adam, when humanity fell into sin, a relational void was created that can be satisfied only by God. He knows you long to connect with Him, so He sent His Son to restore and reconcile what had been marred by sin. He knows you have a longing for eternity, so He offers you a home in His presence for all time.

God delights in you. If you have come to faith in Jesus Christ, the Father is able to interact with you differently than He did before you became a believer. At one point, you lived apart from Him, but now you're a member of His family. When He sees you, He sees His Son living within you. God has the same delight for you as He has for your Bridegroom, Jesus Christ.

God protects and defends you. In this world, there are all kinds of dangers and threats. There's a spiritual battle taking place around us that we don't always perceive. There are physical dangers, threats to our reputations, and other forms of adversity as well. But God hasn't left you to fend for yourself in the midst of this. He cares for you. He protects you. He defends you. And He assures you that the day is coming when you will see Him face to face, live in His presence, and experience the perfect security of His protective care forever.

And sometimes He chooses to reinforce these truths when you're trying to move furniture.

Years ago, I learned an expensive lesson about bearing weight on my own instead of relying on help. When our children were young and we had just moved to a new home, my wife and I decided to buy a new coffee table and end tables that we could use downstairs. We got them at a really fair price, and the furniture store employees even helped me load them into our van. They were large, bulky, and heavy, but they were packed in boxes to protect them from damage.

When I got home, I asked my wife if she would help me carry the boxes into the house. She tried but then set her side of the box down on the ground. "This is too heavy for me. You're going to need to get someone else to help," she said. I assured her that we could do it, but she wouldn't budge. "Get someone else to help you," she insisted.

But I didn't ask someone else for help. Instead, I got mad at my wife and said, "Fine. I'll move these things myself!"

They were too heavy to be carried by one person, which forced me to get creative. I assumed the tables were somewhat cushioned since they were packed in boxes, so I decided to flip the boxes end over end until I got them into the house. Once the boxes were down the steps and into the room, I unpackaged them. One end table was fine, but the other end table and the coffee table were visibly damaged in multiple places.

In my frustration, I tried to do something alone that I should have sought help with. And I paid the price.

Anxiety is a lot like those tables. It's the fruit of trying to carry around things that are too big for one set of arms to lift.

What have you been trying to carry around lately? Is it too big for you emotionally and spiritually? Is it starting to crush you? Would you be willing to accept God's offer to carry it for you?

DWELL ON THIS

I am not designed to bear my burdens alone. Today I can cast my anxiety and worries on God instead of carrying them around myself.

Choose not to be easily provoked by others.

Be not quick in your spirit to
become angry, for anger lodges in
the heart of fools.

—*Ecclesiastes 7:9*

Several months ago on a Sunday morning, I was driving to
church with my sons. We typically try to arrive earlier than
most people so we can get a series of things ready for the
worship service. We turn on the lights, adjust the thermostats,
and take care of a few other odds and ends. I also make a point
to check the mailbox since I'm not usually at the building the
day before when the mail is delivered.

That particular Sunday, there was a handwritten letter in
the mailbox. Seeing something like that was less common
than it had been years ago, so the letter caught my attention. I
wondered if I should read it right then or wait until later in
the day. Admittedly, my curiosity got the best of me and I
opened it.

The letter was written on rather nice stationery and began
with a pleasant greeting. However, the writer proceeded to cut
me down and insult me. The spirit of the letter could be para-

phrased in one sentence: "I don't like you, and it gives me a strange sense of pleasure to attempt to hurt your feelings." Even more painful was the fact that it was written by someone we had just blessed with a small gift of appreciation.

After reading that letter, I felt disturbed all morning. I wished I had waited until later in the day to read it because it affected my ability to greet people and preach. I was annoyed that I allowed the immature and petty words of an unkind man to bother me. As I prayed that evening, the Lord comforted my heart and helped me release the anger and irritation I was feeling.

There are some people in this world who take great delight in provoking you to anger. They're looking for a fight. They want to get under your skin. They clap their hands in glee when they succeed in upsetting you. And it's easy to let them exasperate you, but it isn't wise. You can choose not to be easily provoked by people with poor motives or unhealthy intentions.

I have wrestled with my anger during several seasons of my life. Maybe you can identify. Some of those seasons have been brief. Others were lengthy. None of them were productive. Every time I have allowed myself to be easily provoked to anger, I effectively robbed myself of the privilege that it is to walk in the peace of Christ.

Anger is similar to anxiety. It's triggered by the realization that something is outside our control. We can't control the actions or words of others. We can't control the way people treat us. We can't control many of the circumstances we find ourselves in. So in our weaker moments, we sometimes allow people or circumstances that we can't control to provoke anger within us. That's a regrettable way to handle provocation, as "anger lodges in the heart of fools" (Ecclesiastes 7:9).

Have you ever had company come to visit who overstayed their welcome? A few years ago, my wife and I entertained a visit from some friends that extended much further into the evening than we'd expected. We both had become painfully tired but still wanted to be good hosts. However, it seemed as though our guests had no intention of ever leaving our home. There was one point in which I may have been tempted to draw up a lease agreement and charge them rent. They had "lodged" themselves in our house far beyond the conventions of courtesy. Eventually, Andrea excused herself and went to bed, and I had the awkward task of telling our guests that I was about to do the same. Thankfully, they got the hint.

When people provoke us, the resulting anger can lodge itself in our lives for far too long, much like an unwelcomed houseguest does. It takes up space it shouldn't be using. It conflicts with our ability to rest. It consumes our thinking, sours our food, and dampens our light. And even if we know ahead of time that this is a distinct possibility, we still have a habit of allowing ourselves to be easily aggravated by those who clearly don't have our best intentions at heart.

We have a better option. Through the counsel of God's Word and the presence of His Spirit, we're able to limit the power of the provocations that come our way. Jesus modeled this for us during His time on earth. There were people who provoked Jesus regularly. Religious leaders, government representatives, His brothers, soldiers, and crowds of mockers did their best to hurt and upset Him.

But Jesus didn't take the bait. He didn't play the game on the terms set by those who sought to crush His spirit. He had the power to destroy anyone who attempted to cut Him down, but He chose to restrain it. He kept His power under control while being tormented on the cross. He even asked

God the Father to forgive those who had set themselves against Him, as they truly had no idea what they were doing.

Do you suppose those who have provoked you to anger knew how much their words and deeds upset you? Do you think they were aware of how their hurtful words were making your blood boil or your heart sink? I guess it's possible that some of them may have known they were causing you pain, but I think it's even more likely that they didn't realize just how hurtful their provocation felt to you.

Regardless of their intentions, how does Scripture encourage us to respond? What did Jesus teach us in His moments of pain? God's Word makes it clear that there is no benefit that will come to us by harboring resentment or reacting in anger. Anger, in fact, lodges in the hearts of fools, not in the hearts of the wise or mature.

In my life, there are people who seem to excel at angering me. I tend to feel most provoked when I've been lied to, taken advantage of, or unfairly criticized, or when my time has been intentionally wasted. But what happens if I forget the Lord's counsel when provocation comes? If I act out of anger or harbor bitterness, I'll effectively choose the path of the fool. However, if I make the conscious choice to seek the Lord's strength and respond with forgiveness and grace, my heart will find greater rest, even in the midst of ongoing irritation.

You can't control what others choose to do to you, but with the help of the Holy Spirit, you can control the way you respond. You can respond with grace, mercy, and compassion. Remind yourself that the people who are provoking you are probably experiencing a great deal of pain themselves. It very well may be that they've chosen to irritate you in an effort to share their pain with you because they don't know what else to do with it.

When people intentionally attempt to anger you, they won't be expecting gracious, merciful, or compassionate responses in return. They'll expect you to either cower to their attacks or go on the attack yourself. But the power of Christ enables you to take a different, and often unexpected, approach. You're given the ability to respond in such a way that Christ becomes visible in you.

Sometimes that ability becomes particularly visible through your primary areas of service. As a pastor, I have had plenty of opportunities to practice responding with grace. In my leadership roles, I make decisions, and sometimes people may get mad at me because they don't like them. This is especially true when these people's personal agendas conflict with the teaching of Scripture or with the greater good of God's people. Sometimes these people turn to the silent treatment. More times than I can count on one hand, I have been ignored and not spoken to after making leadership decisions.

Often, I have been tempted to respond in kind by choosing not to engage the person in conversation. After all, he or she will just ignore me, right? But even though I'd feel justified in responding that way, the Holy Spirit speaks to my heart: "That person needs to see Christ in your response. Yes, he is unkind to you and is attempting to rile you up. Respond with joy." So I say hello or wish him a good morning as I pass by, even when I know I'll be ignored.

Even if it goes against your natural response, don't trade provocations with others.

Don't allow someone else's bad attitude to dictate the way you treat him or her.

Don't throw off self-control or dismiss the power Jesus has given you.

Choose not to be easily provoked by others.

DWELL ON THIS

I have been divinely empowered to radiate the joy of
Christ. Therefore, I need to allow others, particularly
those who irritate me, to see and experience Jesus in
me, today and every day.

Listen to those who love you enough to tell you the truth.

Let a righteous man strike me—it
  is a kindness;
    let him rebuke me—it is oil for
    my head;
  let my head not refuse it.

—*Psalm* 141:5

While I was in college, I managed an on-campus eatery. The place had just opened, and I oversaw operations several nights each week. A student about ten years older than I was had been hired to work the same shift. Naturally speaking, there was a part of me that felt as though I needed to defer to him in certain areas because of our age difference, but practically speaking, I was in charge and needed to keep things running smoothly.

Over time, it became clear to me that my coworker was lazy. Whenever possible, he would walk out into the dining area, sit down, and watch television. At first I didn't say much about it to him. I kept waiting for him to realize he was creating more work for me when he took frequent and unnecessary breaks. But that didn't happen. He continued taking advantage of the fact that I was shouldering most of the work.

I decided to seek advice from my father. He owned a grocery store and had hired many employees over the years. I knew he would identify with my situation, as he had dealt with bad or unproductive employees in the past. I figured he would be sympathetic when I complained to him about my employee.

Guess what? He wasn't. When I told him what was going on, he said, "It sounds to me like you're a bad manager."

Ouch.

This wasn't what I wanted to hear. I wanted him to pat me on the back, tell me that he understood, and let me vent for a little while. When he gave me a blunt response instead, I felt insulted. My feelings were hurt, and I regretted telling him about the situation. In retrospect, I can see my dad was giving me great advice. He was trying to help me realize that if I wore the title manager, I needed to do a better job of managing inefficient and lazy employees. His advice hurt in the moment, but what he said was true, and the lesson I learned from that conversation has served me well throughout my adult life.

The truth can be painful, but it is a good thing. It's easier to live in a fantasy of falsehood and self-deception than to own up to the truth. It has become culturally commonplace to lie to one another because we think it's polite. After all, it can hurt to hear the truth. I've learned this is especially true in the United States. Several years ago, I visited a friend whose wife grew up in Germany. They had invited some of their German friends (who had just moved to the United States) to join us for dinner. One of their friends worked for BMW and had recently completed training that was designed to help him assimilate into American culture. Intrigued, I asked him what he was taught in the training and he said, "One of the things they told us was that you can't always take what Americans say at face value. For instance, someone might say, 'Let's grab lunch together sometime soon!' but he might not mean it. You'll be tempted to start selecting a date in your calendar, but an American would instinctively know that the other person was just being polite and might not actually want to meet for lunch."

Although it's hard to hear, his training was spot-on. We say things we don't mean all the time because we value appearing friendly more than we value being a true friend. We value being polite more than we value being honest. And since that's the case, we often begin to resent those who love us enough to tell us the truth.

King David, on the other hand, knew the value of honesty. Kings and prominent leaders are always surrounded by yes-men and those who want to curry their favor—because who would want to irritate or upset a government leader who had the power to take your life? I imagine that David frequently asked himself, *Is this person giving me honest counsel, or is he just telling me what he thinks I want to hear?* Without the help of the Holy Spirit, that would be rather difficult to discern.

David was blessed with several people in his life who took the risk to tell him painfully honest things. As he grew in wisdom, David was able to say, "Let a righteous man strike me— it is a kindness" (Psalm 141:5). He became keenly aware that the truth was hard to come by and that even if it felt like a slap to the face, it was really a blessing and an act of kindness.

David viewed the rebuke of a righteous man as "oil for

[his] head" (verse 5). He rejoiced in honest words because he knew that a moment of sharp correction could save him from a lifetime of painful consequences.

Why do we resent those who tell us the truth? Is it because we try to validate our sense of self-worth through a perfect lens? We cast an image in our minds of how we hope to be perceived, and we expect nothing less than perfection. When someone finds a crack in that mirror, we feel attacked. It is hard to admit we made a mistake, and even harder when others point out our flaws to us. Their honesty competes with our desire to affirm our preconceived image of ourselves.

If we tie our sense of worth to that image, we can begin to drift in an unhealthy direction. We will embrace shallow falsehoods, and we might even forget that our value is derived from our relationships with Christ. After all, we were created in His image. Through faith, we are united to Him. We are welcomed into His family, and He never hesitates to tell us the truth.

Why is Jesus honest with us? It's because He loves us. I wonder, though, do we ever resent His honesty as well? When you're reading the Bible and Jesus confronts you with something you didn't want to hear, what do you do with that information? Do you continue to live as though you'd never read it, or do you embrace the truth and thank Him for lovingly throwing a cup of cold water in your face?

As a pastor who regularly counsels people, I see a variety of reactions when I confront people with the very things they need to hear. Some run away. Some get angry. Some tell me I'm wrong. Some ignore what I say. But others embrace the truth.

There are millions of people in this world who would rather suffer with their issues and create long-lasting problems for themselves and others than experience a moment of admitting painful truths so they can begin the process of healing.

Has the Lord blessed you with a few honest people in your life? Do you find yourself gravitating toward them or running from them? Do you hide from the truth? Or have you learned, as David did, that those who tell you the truth are some of the best friends you will ever have?

Don't resent those who are honest with you. Don't hide in your house for months on end because you're afraid of hearing what you'd rather not hear. Don't ignore calls and texts. Don't medicate your emotional pain with something that's going to produce pain in a different area of your life. Instead, search for the kindness in the rebuke. Learn to admit the truth to yourself and give thanks for the truth tellers.

Many people in your life care more about whether you think they're "nice" than about telling you the truth.

Many people in your life are willing to watch you suffer because they fear the repercussions of being honest with you.

If you're blessed, there are those in your life who will risk their esteem in your eyes to tell you the truth. Don't resent them. They are evidence of God's favor toward you. Joyfully give thanks to Him for blessing you with their honesty. Listen to their counsel when God is speaking to you through them.

DWELL ON THIS

> Today I will listen to those who love me enough to tell me the truth, even if the message stings.

Make the most of your privilege to repent.

Do you presume on the riches of his kindness and forbearance and patience, not knowing that God's kindness is meant to lead you to repentance?

—*Romans* 2:4

I can remember being easily scared when I was a child. My active daytime imagination fashioned all kinds of frightening scenarios that turned into nightmares when I slept. At one point, my nightmares became so intense that my parents tried to protect me from all sorts of things that they thought might terrify me. Their efforts were well intentioned but didn't work. All these years later, I still remember some of those dreams in vivid detail and can understand why they would have produced fear in me.

As I grew older, I learned to confront my fears by intentionally creating scenarios that forced me to interact with what I was afraid of. This sounds funny to admit now, but when I was a child one of my biggest fears was that ventriloquist dummies were actually alive and might be prone to murder unsuspecting people. I had dreams about being attacked by them, and the very sight of them when I was awake creeped me out, so I decided to do something about it.

One evening while I was walking through a toy store with my father and my sisters, I came across a display of ventriloquist dummies for sale. Even though those things freaked me out, I asked my father to buy one for me. He declined my request but was then forced to put up with incessant requests over the next six weeks. Finally, he agreed to purchase it for me, and I brought it home.

Though both fascinated and terrified, I was determined to learn how to use it. I read the book that came with it and practiced speaking without moving my lips, but I still maintained a fear that the dummy might actually come to life and kill me. I knew that the fear was irrational, yet I still wrestled with it.

In my room, I had a rocking chair directly across from my bed. Instead of packing that dummy away in a box when I finished practicing, I would set it upright on that chair, where I could see it when I went to bed. It looked as if it were staring at me, but I tried to resist the urge to freak out.

One evening while I was feeling somewhat weak and fearful, I walked over to the dummy and stared at it. Then I said, "I know you're alive." I fully expected it to move, especially because I had exposed its secret. After a few seconds of waiting, I abruptly raised my right hand and slapped the dummy in the face. I'm not sure if I was trying to assert my dominance or convince myself I wasn't terrified, but that's what I did, and then I stood back and waited to see what would happen. Still nothing, so I went to bed. And, obviously, the dummy didn't kill me that night or any other.

I know how ridiculous my actions sound, but in that moment, I confronted my irrational fear and began the process of reducing its power over me.

I laugh when I tell people that story now, but there's also a part of me that is pleased with what took place during that season of my life. I was transitioning from being a frightened boy into someone who chose to confront my fears. I learned at a young age that I preferred to overcome my fears instead of being overcome by them, and I've seen this pattern repeated in my adult life.

So, fellow adult, what are you afraid of? What are you doing with that fear?

If you need help coming up with an answer, let me help you. Would you like to hear a scary word? Yes? Okay, here it is: repent!

I'm convinced that repentance is one of the most fear-inducing and misunderstood concepts for many Christians. We hear that word and we're immediately put on the defense. It sounds scary and confrontational. Hearing the word repent conjures up mental images of a smug religious fanatic screaming it in our face or a cluster of protesters waving the word around on homemade signs.

But true repentance isn't scary or combative; it's beautiful, beneficial, and helpful. When practiced, it can calm our worries, relieve our guilt, and foster healthy restoration between offending parties. Repentance is a privilege of Christ's followers, yet many of us don't take advantage of it because we're afraid of it, we don't understand it, or we're too proud to use it.

In the second chapter of Romans, Paul lovingly reprimanded those who were steeped in their self-seeking pride and disobedience: "Do you presume on the riches of his kindness and forbearance and patience, not knowing that God's kindness is meant to lead you to repentance?" (verse 4). He confronted the fruit of rebellion with the fruit of obedience. He drew a bold contrast between embracing the heart of this world and the heart of God.

Paul gives us a powerful picture of God's character in that verse. He tells us that God is kind, shows restraint, and is patient. I admire people who display those qualities, because of how difficult it is to consistently lead with those traits. Yet they are aspects of God's nature that He exhibits toward us every single day.

It's easy to try to exploit God's kindness, misapply His tolerance or patience, or persist in sin. We're so used to the Lord showing incredible restraint. However, God isn't being kind to us so we can develop a habit of taking advantage of Him; His kindness is meant to lead us to repentance.

Because God is genuinely kind by nature, we should come to understand that it's safe to repent. He knows we need to, so He makes it inviting for us to do so. It's safe because we're coming to the One who loves us deeply and His love for us isn't fickle.

But what does it mean to repent? Is it a onetime event, or is it an ongoing practice? Is repenting something we do when we're immature but have less of a need to do once we're grown?

Biblical repentance involves turning away from something and toward something else. When we repent, we're turning from our old beliefs to our new beliefs. We're turning from worldliness to godliness. We're turning from wrath to mercy. We're turning from Christlessness to Christlikeness.

At the moment we come to faith in Christ, we repent. We're repenting from the false belief that we are fine on our own, and we're embracing the fact that we are sinners in need of the Savior. We're rejecting our ignorance of forgiveness and embracing the complete pardon that Jesus offers us. We're withdrawing from hopelessness and embracing the hope Christ supplies. We're renouncing the use of sin to satisfy the longings of our souls and embracing the peace of Christ, which brings us rest.

Repentance isn't something worth embracing only the day we come to faith in Christ; we're encouraged to practice it throughout our Christian lives as we struggle with sin and false beliefs. We wrestle with those things daily, but we don't need to be overcome by them. As the Holy Spirit reveals our false beliefs and sinful practices, we can safely confess to Him and repent of them. We don't need to hide our struggles; we can openly and fearlessly admit them in the presence of our kind God.

Repenting also frees us from depending on ourselves or bragging. We don't have to try to pretend we're perfect. Our sense of self-worth is not found in others' perceptions of us. As we become familiar with confessing and repenting of our sin before the Lord, we become more comfortable in admitting our struggles to each other. I see this play out in my home quite regularly.

I seem to create plenty of opportunities for repentance. A few days ago, I yelled at my son for spilling salt all over our kitchen table and floor. Well, technically, I didn't yell at him for that; I yelled at him for the way he was attempting to clean it up. He was making more of a mess than I thought he needed to, and I spoke harshly to him. I wasn't really that mad, but I could tell I chose my words and tone poorly. I was abrupt and needlessly hurt his feelings. The very next day, I cut my wife off midconversation. It annoyed and insulted her.

In both cases, I was careless with how I spoke and could have allowed both of those offenses to linger without apologizing for them. But because the Lord is teaching me that it's safe to repent to Him, I'm also learning that it's safe to repent to others. My wife and son didn't think less of me when I apologized. They respected me more because I showed them I truly do care for their feelings.

Jesus is perfect; I'm not. Someday—in heaven—I will be, but while I'm in this earthly body, I'm still in the process of growing. I'm learning new things. The Lord is teaching me more about relying on Him daily. He's showing me that it's better to admit my struggles to Him than it is to live as if I don't have any. If I convince myself that my sin isn't really sin or isn't really that much of an issue, I won't repent. I'll turn toward sin and away from Christ, and eventually I'll regret doing so when I experience the consequences.

Are you making the most of your opportunity to repent? Do you truly believe that the Lord is kind and patient with His children? If He made a point to emphasize His kindness and patience in Scripture, shouldn't we start allowing ourselves to see Him through that lens?

Are there any false beliefs that have crept into your life that the Lord is inviting you to repent of?

Are there any actions you've taken or sins you've participated in that the Lord is inviting you to turn from so you can embrace Him more fully?

You have been given the privilege to repent. The Lord invites you to make repentance a dominant facet of your life.

DWELL ON THIS

Repentance isn't terrifying; it's a privilege that Jesus is calling me to make the most of today and every day.

God's goodness and mercy are pursuing you.

Surely goodness and mercy shall
found me
all the days of my life,
and I shall dwell in the house of
the LORD
forever.

—*Psalm* 23:6

My sister has a little dog named Gracie. I'd love to tell you that Gracie is friendly and endears herself to people, but if I did that, I would need to repent of my dishonesty. When my sister hosts family events and parties, Gracie avoids everyone except my sister. Occasionally, she will emerge to bark and growl at people, but most of the time, she hides.

Recently, my sister and her family were preparing to take a short vacation, so she asked my father if he would watch Gracie for a few days at his house. He agreed, but he knew it was going to be a challenge. I called and asked him how things were going, and he said, "Well, for the most part Gracie just stands on the back of my couch, staring out the window, waiting for your sister to come back and rescue her. The other day, however, she escaped and I was worried she might not come back."

My father is older now, so none of us would expect him to chase Gracie through the neighborhood if she ran away. But I have no doubt that forty years ago, he would have done just that. In fact, he still bears the scars of a dog chase that didn't go quite as he'd expected.

Many years ago, after my grandparents' dog died, my father and his brothers thought it would be a good idea to surprise them with a new dog. My grandparents liked German shepherds, so my dad and uncles bought them one named Duchess. I'm not positive, but I'm pretty sure Duchess was insane.

My grandparents were excellent with dogs, but nothing seemed to calm Duchess down. She jumped on everyone, chewed on everything, barked continually, fought other creatures, and had a not-so-secret desire to be an Olympic sprinter.

One summer evening when we were visiting my grandparents, Duchess made a break for it. She was on a leash but darted away when the grip wasn't firm. She went on a running spree of the East Mountain community in Scranton, Pennsylvania. Not wanting my grandparents to have to endure the pain of losing another dog, my father went running after Duchess.

My dad isn't an athlete or a stuntman, but I think he became both that day. In dress shoes and slacks, he darted up the street as fast as he could run. Duchess must have thought it was a game to see him chasing her. She would come close to him, then sprint away. He'd run some more and make a swipe at her leash as it was flapping in the wind, but she kept eluding him.

Finally, after many minutes of being chased, she stopped. Something else grabbed her attention. In a nearby yard, there were two dogs tethered to a post. Duchess looked at them and started to growl. It was clear she was poised to attack them, so my father knew he needed to intervene quickly. Taking advantage of her momentary pause, he mustered up all his energy and dove at her.

Success! He grabbed the leash and held her secure. Unfortunately, he also succeeded in smashing his face on the pavement and breaking his four front teeth in half. He brought Duchess back to my grandparents' yard, but his clothes were filthy, his teeth were missing, his face was covered in sweat and blood, and he was about to owe his dentist over three thousand dollars.

Duchess was crazy, yet we're all a lot like her. We bark when we shouldn't. We gnaw at things until they're ruined. We risk our safety by running when we're supposed to remain still, and we pick fights even when we're outnumbered. Yet Jesus pursues us anyway, and He doesn't regret the cost He incurred, the blood He shed, or the clothing that was torn from Him in the midst of the pursuit.

Our Lord is the perfection of goodness. He is likewise the perfection of faithful love and mercy. He cares deeply for us and seeks us when we take off running. Psalm 23:6 tells us that God's goodness and faithful love are pursuing us. The Lord is actively doing this, not just passively allowing it.

It can be easy at times to convince ourselves that we are overlooked or not valuable. Sometimes we think our "crazy" is too off-putting for God to want to show us His goodness. Yet His Word tells us otherwise—that He is rushing toward us with goodness and mercy.

Psalm 23 provides a beautiful picture of the gentle care the Lord shows His children, like a shepherd caring for sheep. It's a portion of Scripture that many people have memorized line for line.

Why is it that we can spend our whole lives reading a portion of Scripture about the mercy of God yet fail to show each other mercy?

Why is it that we can commit every word of Psalm 23 to memory but doubt that the Lord would actually apply His mercy to our lives?

Why is it that we can tell our children that God loves them enough to pursue them with His goodness and mercy yet we question whether He is willing to be the same way toward us?

Throughout our lives, we're going to have all kinds of experiences. We're going to have moments when we feel that everything is wonderful and life can't get any better, and we're also going to have moments that devastate us. The pain will feel unbearable. We may even want to retreat from being around others for fear that they will hurt us more than we can tolerate.

In those times, it can be easy to forget that God is pursuing us with His goodness, love, and mercy. I think that's a big reason why we also struggle to show mercy to others. We struggle to show it because we forget that we're receiving it. God is pursuing us with goodness and mercy, and according to Psalm 23:6, He's been doing that our entire lives.

We love to say "God is good!" when we find something we lost or when one of our children gets offered a prestigious job, but can we also say "God is good!" with the same level of enthusiasm when our kids rebel, our friends reject us, or we're feeling depressed?

If what the Lord reveals to us in Psalm 23 is true, that means He is pursuing us with goodness, love, and mercy all the days of our lives, in every context we will ever find ourselves. He is chasing us down in our low moments. He's celebrating with us in our high moments. And He's so intentional about the direction our lives take that He's orchestrating all our circumstances in such a way that we'll be able to gain a greater glimpse of His goodness if we allow ourselves to start seeing with His eyes.

God is good to us now, and He assures us that His goodness toward His children will extend eternally. There will never be a time when He will relent from pursuing us with it. Not today. Not ever.

How often do you tell yourself that God is pursuing you with His goodness and mercy? Is this something you've ever told yourself? I'm not just asking if you believe that God is good and merciful; I want to know if you truly believe He's actively and lovingly hunting you down with perfect goodness, mercy, and love.

Tell yourself that God is being good to you today, even if you're still struggling to see where or how.

Tell yourself that God is mercifully chasing you down so you don't get torn apart by whatever unhealthy thing has grabbed your attention.

Tell yourself that God is willing to look past your craziness and still call you His child.

Tell yourself that God loves you enough to make a spectacle of Himself chasing you through mountains and ditches so He can bring you safely home into His presence forever.

DWELL ON THIS

God's goodness and mercy are actively pursuing me today and every day.

You can take refuge in God.

Oh, taste and see that the LORD is
good!
Blessed is the man who takes
refuge in him!

—*Psalm 34:8*

Have you ever been chased by a cop? If you haven't, I don't recommend giving it a try. But when I was in ninth grade, I made a habit of it. I wish I were kidding, but I'm not.

I've lived in several places in northeastern Pennsylvania but spent most of my youth in the city of Carbondale. Carbondale is a unique place. When I lived there, it had a population of around nine thousand people, which might make you wonder why it was called a city. After living there for nine years, the best answer I can give you is that if Carbondale wants to be called a city, it's a city, and you'd be wise not to press the issue.

I liked living in Carbondale. Several friends who lived in surrounding towns have told me that they always thought of it as being a tougher place to grow up than other places in

Lackawanna County. I guess there might be some truth to that, but when you live there, you learn to adapt.

Our family moved to Carbondale right before I started fourth grade. At my old school in Peckville, there weren't many playground fights. In Carbondale, there were fights nearly every day. When I was the new kid, I was regularly on the receiving end of the combat. I didn't know how to fight when I moved there, but I quickly learned. Once I finally won a few, I guess the rest of the guys thought I was sufficiently initiated into the community, and I went from being an outsider to being accepted by my peers. I really didn't have too many problems after that.

During our early teen years, before we owned cars, my friends and I used to wander the streets of Carbondale constantly. Sometimes I wonder how many miles a day we must have walked. I'm certain it was significant. As we wandered around town, we would frequently run into other friends, and there was a fifty-fifty chance we would either play basketball or get in minor trouble with the police. Even when we weren't looking for trouble, it seemed the police assumed we were likely to make it (which was a safe assumption), so they would "check in" with us to see what we were up to.

I'll never forget one evening when my friend Mike and I were walking through town on one of the streets that intersected with Eighth Avenue. We weren't causing trouble or making a scene that evening; we were just walking around because we didn't have anything better to do.

As we walked, we could hear the sound of a car in the distance. It sounded as if it were driving quickly up Eighth Avenue, and when it passed the intersection of the street we were on, it slammed on its brakes, reversed direction, and came flying toward us. It was a police car, and it was clear they had seen us and thought we must have done something, so they tried to catch us, and we instinctively ran.

Mike and I immediately darted between two houses and ran through a backyard. It was dark, but I could see there was an old fence at the end of the property, separating it from the house behind it. I was planning to climb the fence, but Mike ran straight into it so hard that he knocked it down, which placed us in the backyard of a house on the parallel street from where we had started.

At this point, the police were exiting their car and getting ready to chase us on foot. We didn't have much of a lead on them, so we needed to act quickly. Leaning against the house was a medium-sized plastic kiddie pool that was probably placed there so it could drain. I grabbed Mike's arm and pulled him behind that pool, where I hoped we could hide from the cops. We could hear them running, so I whispered to Mike, "Don't even breathe!"

We sat crouched behind that pool for several tense minutes. Merely feet away, we could hear the police walking around and talking to the homeowner whose fence we had just crashed through. The light from flashlights was shining all around us, but no one thought to look behind that plastic pool. If they had, they would have easily nabbed us.

At last, we stopped hearing footsteps and could no longer see signs of flashlights. Mike and I waited for a few additional minutes until we were convinced that no one was around, and then we got out of there as quickly as we could. For a tense five-minute span of time, that plastic pool was our place of refuge. It was the only thing separating us from the threat of punishment, whether we deserved it or not.

Everyone craves a place of safety and protection. Scripture reveals to us that we can obtain ultimate safety and a place of refuge in God. For those who trust in Him, He serves as our protector, defender, and overseer. We are safe in His compassionate hands.

But that's a perspective we usually learn to embrace after we've been threatened, not before. It usually takes experiencing the exhaustion of running and hiding for us to realize that worldly sources of refuge are as flimsy as a plastic kiddie pool. One small gust of wind or the tap of a flashlight can knock that thing over and expose us to capture.

The Lord wants us to be convinced that He is a refuge for us.

He shelters us from pursuit.

He shelters us from danger.

He shelters us from trouble.

In the Bible, we see that David learned these lessons in a powerful way throughout his life. Scripture tells of multiple instances when David was being pursued by those who were intent on capturing him and taking his life. At one point, when he was running from King Saul, he fled to the city of Gath (1 Samuel 21:10). But wherever David ran, he had a hard time escaping his reputation.

In Gath, the servants of King Achish were nervous about welcoming David into their midst (verse 11). They knew he was a man of power and influence. His many successes demonstrated that God's hand was upon him, and they were fearful that he might actually harm them. They expressed this concern to Achish, and David caught wind of their comments, so he hatched a plan. In some respects, it was a weak plan, but in David's estimation, it must have been the best option he could come up with on short notice.

We're told that David changed his behavior in front of the king and his servants and pretended to be insane. He let spit and slobber run down his beard. He scratched at the doors of the gate like a man desperate for refuge, not a man of power or prestige. When the king saw him, he dismissed him as just another loon. I always get a kick out of Achish's comments in verse 15: "Am I so short of madmen that you have to bring this fellow here to carry on like this in front of me?" (NIV). David didn't seem like a threat at all, so Achish let him be.

I'm able to find that story comical because it ended well, and I imagine it may have given David a chuckle from time to time when he told that story later in life. But in the moment, I don't think David found it funny at all. His life was genuinely threatened. In one direction, he was being hunted by Saul, who was bent on killing him. And if Achish wanted to, he could have killed David on the spot. But instead, David did a little acting, and the Lord prompted Achish to view him as a harmless nuisance, not a threat.

It was with these events in mind that David composed Psalm 34. There he said, "Oh, taste and see that the LORD is good! Blessed is the man who takes refuge in him!" (verse 8). David had enough experiences with the Lord at that point to allow him to get a "taste" of what He likes to do in the life of someone who trusts Him completely.

The Lord is abundantly good to His children. He delights in helping us realize He is the place of refuge to which we should run. It's never safe to run from Him, but it's always wise to run to Him. David was freshly reminded of this after his interaction with Achish was over, and he joyfully praised the Lord for being a refuge for him in the midst of threats and pursuit.

The Lord is your refuge as well. When was the last time you told yourself you can take refuge in Him? In your seasons of trouble, threat, and despair, where have you been trying to find shelter?

Several years ago, I went through a season of painful discouragement. In the midst of that despair, my heart was craving a place of sanctuary. I needed a break from stress, criticism, and emotional overload. In search of refuge, I did several things, all of which were nice but inadequate. I spent time tucked away in my basement on a comfy couch, I took random road trips to some of my favorite places, and I treated myself to a leadership conference in Florida.

I don't think any of those options were bad, but they certainly weren't sufficient. It wasn't until I began reminding myself that the Lord wanted me to seek refuge in Him that I started to feel better. Only He could fully heal my hurting heart.

What sources of refuge have you enjoyed, only to be forced to admit they were inadequate? Do you find refuge in solitude? Movies? Sports? Food? Music? Vacations? Shopping? Hobbies? Other distractions? A source of refuge that takes our focus off God isn't a refuge at all. It's an idol, and idols can't help us because they don't love us back.

Tell yourself to taste and see that the Lord is good.

Tell yourself that He blesses those who go to Him for refuge.

Tell yourself that He won't leave you disappointed as your idols have because, unlike them, He loves you back.

DWELL ON THIS

> When I'm seeking a place of shelter, protection, and defense, I can take refuge in God.

DAY 14

God wipes your slate clean.

If we confess our sins, he is faithful
and just to forgive us our sins and
to cleanse us from all
unrighteousness.

—1 John 1:9

Early in our marriage, Andrea and I decided it would be a good idea to develop more than one stream of income. Before we had children, she taught at a Christian school. That was a huge help to our household budget because I didn't have a very impressive individual paycheck. But when our first child was born, my wife transitioned out of her job so she could stay home. We were both supportive of this idea, but the loss of her income meant our budget was going to be cut in half.

At the time, I wanted to figure out a way to replace her income, allow her to stay home with our daughter (and future siblings who were born in rapid succession), and do so in a way that my responsibilities and time commitments as a pastor wouldn't be hindered.

I researched a few options but kept coming back to real estate. We were in our early twenties and lived in a church parsonage, so we didn't have any experience buying property, but I got an idea in my head that I thought might work. I suggested to Andrea that we buy a cottage in the Pocono Mountains and rent it out to families on vacation. She was intrigued by the idea, especially after I called a few similar properties while pretending to be a prospective renter. In the process, I learned that those properties were booked solid. I did the math and realized we could also turn a nice profit if we gave this idea a try.

We called a real estate agent and began touring various properties. Although many of them were in nice shape, their prices were a little too steep for our budget. But one of the homes was very affordable, and we asked our agent to take us to see it.

The home was a three-bedroom, three-bathroom sixteen-hundred-square-foot chalet in a gated community. It had been foreclosed on several months earlier and was just sitting there abandoned. When the agent unlocked the door, we quickly saw why the house was as affordable as it was. It was filthy. Every room was piled high with abandoned garbage, and several water pipes had frozen and cracked. In addition to that, the place smelled terrible.

My wife is wonderful, and I truly appreciate her willingness to participate in the crazy ideas I come up with—like this one. After discussing our options, we decided to make an offer on the house and attempt to fix it ourselves. Our offer was accepted, and we got to work.

Truckload after truckload of garbage, carpet, old appliances, and abandoned belongings were removed from the house. Then we thoroughly cleaned it from top to bottom. We fixed the pipes, repaired the chimney, replaced the appliances, updated the flooring, painted the walls, replaced the sewage ejection pump, added auxiliary propane heaters, and corrected some wiring issues. We stained the deck, painted the siding, and planted new landscaping to add curb appeal. Whatever we couldn't do ourselves, we paid professionals to do or we utilized the help of knowledgeable family members.

Once all the work was done, we furnished the home, decorated it, and took pictures that we could use to market it online. Then we waited to see if anyone would rent it. My grandfather thought we were in over our heads. My uncle told me I was making a mistake. My father was excited for me but still skeptical (and probably wondering if I'd ask him to bail me out if it all flopped).

Within days of placing our ad online, the calls started coming in, and before we knew it, we were raising our rates and turning away renters because available dates had filled. My supportive but skeptical family members were all amazed, as were we. In the end, the income from that property not only replaced my wife's lost salary but also doubled it.

One of the things I'm extremely grateful we had the foresight to do in the midst of that project was take pictures. We have a photo album dedicated to "before and after" pictures taken from all the same angles so we could compare them side by side. All these years later, I'm still amazed when I look at the transformation that took place with that home. When we bought it, the bank that owned it practically wanted to give the filthy dump away. After we renovated it, we had to create a waiting list of all the people who wanted to pay us top dollar just for the privilege of living in it for a week.

That vacation chalet holds some similarities to the work the Lord is doing in our lives. Maybe you've also felt filthy, filled with garbage, and abandoned because of the presence of sin in your life. The burden of sin is too much for any of us to bear. There are mistakes and acts of rebellion in our pasts that can at times haunt our memories and clutter our lives with regret.

But God offers to cleanse us of our sin. He offers to wipe our slates clean and reminds us that as He does so, we can begin to see ourselves from His perspective. In Christ, we are made holy. In Christ, we are made clean.

The Lord can see beyond our messes and beyond our clutter. He can see our value, even if everyone else is skeptical. When God the Father looks at those of us who believe, He sees Jesus Christ, His Son, within us. And in view of the fact that Christ atoned for our sin, God cleanses us of sin when we mistakenly (or rebelliously) invite it back into our lives. He made us new creations in Christ, and He provides ongoing cleansing as we struggle with sin in the midst of this fallen world.

In 1 John 1:9, we're told, "If we confess our sins, he is faithful and just to forgive us our sins and to cleanse us from all unrighteousness." The Lord encourages us to openly admit what He already knows. He invites us to come before Him and confess our sin because it loses its power and allure when it's exposed to the light of His holiness.

When we bought that chalet and fixed it up, our relationship with that building didn't end once the property was restored. Yes, it looked new, but it wouldn't have continued to look that way if we hadn't cared for it and cleaned it on a regular basis. Guests enjoyed staying there, but they also made messes. They damaged what we were invested in, so we had to continue laboring to care for it.

In the chalet, we had a guest book that visitors could sign and in which they could share a little about their vacations. Before I learned how to properly screen guests, I made the mistake of renting the place to a group of guys who left it in terrible condition. One of the guys even signed the guest book, "Nice place! We wrecked it!" Needless to say, I didn't return their damage deposit.

Another guest called me in panic mode on the first day of her visit. She said, "Water is spraying everywhere! It's all over the floors. It's dripping through the vents and flowing through the ceiling. We don't know how to stop it! This isn't something we can fix." Then she screamed the best excuse I ever heard for a lack of plumbing knowledge: "My husband works in computers!"

I called a plumber, and we both rushed to the property only to discover that the residents had caused a toilet to overflow and that's where the water came from. All that panic for a plugged toilet. I paid the plumber fifty dollars for coming out, thanked him for his professional diagnosis of the clog, and helped clean up the mess. The house was nice, but it clearly wasn't going to stay nice on its own.

If we've come to know Christ, we have been made new, but the Lord's relationship with us didn't end when He made us new creations. It's an ongoing relationship. Through His Spirit, He is sanctifying us. He is producing holiness in our lives as He walks us through this process of growth, during which we continually remain dependent on Him for cleansing.

At this point, it's easier for me to excuse the sins of my youth that occurred before I came to faith in Christ, but it's much more difficult for me to move beyond my sin in the present. When I rebel against the Lord, I feel terrible about it. Sometimes it takes a few hours or maybe a day for the gravity of my rebellion to really become clear to me, but when it does, I don't feel so good.

People tend to do one of three things when they aren't

feeling too good about their sin: they pretend it didn't happen, they tell themselves that it wasn't actually sin, or they admit their errors and make different decisions in the future. Sin has the capacity to remain a dominant force in our lives because we ignore it and hide it instead of confessing it and gaining victory over it.

The Lord wants us to confess our sin to Him—not so we'll feel worse about it, but so we won't be controlled by it. He cleanses us of the sin we confess and grieves over the sin we cherish. Jesus came to this earth to liberate us from our slavery to sin. Confession is the process by which the shackles of sin are smashed and we're set free to live in liberty.

The sin you've confessed to the Lord isn't a garment you need to continually wear. He doesn't still see you as the liar, thief, or adulterer you once were. He sees you as you are. He sees what He has remade you to be. You belong to Him. You are His. You have been redeemed through Christ, who already paid for every mistake you've ever made.

Tell yourself that the sin you've confessed is no longer your master.

Tell yourself that God is faithful to you and won't let unrighteousness win the day.

Tell yourself that in Christ, you have been made clean.

DWELL ON THIS

Today I will remind myself that I am no longer defined by unrighteousness and that God has wiped my slate clean.

DAY 15

The Lord will keep His promises to you.

Let us hold fast the confession of
our hope without wavering, for he
who promised is faithful.

—Hebrews 10:23

I don't know who first said it, but I once heard a statement
that I believe is true: "If you want to be respected, always do
what you said you were going to do." That's not a complicated
thought, but how often is it practiced? Even though it may be
difficult to live up to that standard perfectly, it's one of the
guiding principles behind how I try to lead and make decisions. It's also a value that's practiced by the leaders I respect
most.

My eyes were first opened to this principle in childhood.
When I was a kid, I participated in a summer day camp that I
quickly grew to detest.

At the start of the summer, my camp counselor took us to
the various activities that were taking place around the campground. We participated in sports and field games. We swam
in the lake. We made arts and crafts. I even remember liking
the food. But partway through the summer, it became clear to

me that my counselor had shifted to doing the bare minimum to get through the day, and the camp leaders didn't hold him accountable for it. He didn't seem to enjoy working with kids, and he stopped taking us to the different events and activities around the campground. Instead, he would just make us march in the woods for hours every single day.

Don't get me wrong. I like hiking; it's one of my favorite things to do. But that's not what we were doing. After breakfast, we were forced to march in a straight line in one direction and then turn around to march right back to camp in time for lunch. After lunch, we'd head out and march all over again. Single file. No talking. This happened day after day, even though we were promised we'd be allowed to participate in the other activities.

After repeating this process many days in a row and becoming convinced that our counselor had no intention of keeping his promise to allow us to join the rest of the campers, I made the decision that I wasn't going back. That thought consoled me throughout the day as I marched through the woods one final time. I mentioned it to only one other person: the woman who oversaw arts and crafts. A few minutes before we were supposed to get on the buses to head home, I stopped by her station and asked if I could have the tie-dyed shirt I'd made at the start of the summer. She found it for me and asked why I needed it right that second. That's when I told her my secret: "I'm never coming back to this place again."

My counselor didn't keep his promises, but I kept mine. I never again set foot on that property. When I got home that day, I informed my mother of my decision. She was not happy about it, but she could tell I was serious. She said to me, "If you don't get on that bus and go to camp tomorrow, you're going to spend all day pulling weeds. You'll be picking weeds for many hours, in the hot sun, without a break." And I replied, "That works for me. It sounds better than another day of marching."

When I joyfully spent the next day pulling every weed in sight, my mother realized how much I detested those marches at the day camp and didn't force me to go back.

Our camp counselor left us feeling disliked and demoralized. He also taught us not to trust or respect him because he didn't keep his word. I had thought his behavior was an anomaly. Most of the adults in my life up to that point kept their promises, so I didn't really think honesty or follow-through were issues very many grown-ups struggled with. Sadly, my experiences as an adult have taught me otherwise. Would it sound cynical if I admitted that I'm now more surprised when people do exactly what they say they are going to do than when they don't?

What about God's follow-through? All throughout His Word, God makes promises to us. But because we're so used to promises being broken, we can develop a bad habit of questioning the validity of His promises as well.

Do you ever question what God has said?

Do you believe He will fulfill His promises to you?

Many of the promises of God probably seem outlandish to those who don't have a relationship with Him. I'm sure His promises seem like nothing more than creative fantasies to those who doubt the validity of the Bible.

Consider what God has told us in the pages of His Word: He promises to credit righteousness to our account if we trust in Jesus Christ (Romans 4:22–24). He promises to give us rest from our burdens (Matthew 11:28). He promises to create a new heaven and earth that will never be tainted by sin again (Isaiah 65:17). He promises to give believers incorrupt-

ible bodies like Jesus displayed after His resurrection (1 Corinthians 15:53). He promises that Jesus will return to earth to
reign as King (Revelation 19:11–16). He promises to answer
our prayers in accordance with His will (1 John 5:14). He
promises that His will is good, pleasing, and perfect (Romans
12:2). He promises us an inheritance in His kingdom (Ephesians 1:11). And He promises to reward believers who suffer
for the sake of the gospel (1 Peter 3:14).

Which of those do you believe? Which do you question?
What difference does it make if you choose to live as if those
promises are true? What will change in your life if you doubt
the truth of these assertions?

God keeps His promises, and I try to as well. In fact, a big
part of why being a father has been a positive experience for
me comes back to the fact that my children believe me when
I say something. If I tell them I'm taking them somewhere on
vacation, they pack their bags. If I tell them I'll be picking
them up at eleven, they're waiting for me at eleven. If I tell
them that I love them, they believe me because I have kept my
promises to them from the day they were born. Many years of
trust have been accumulated during that time, and having
their trust makes the process of parenting more enjoyable.

I also desire to be a pastor with integrity. I have been leading our church long enough to have a healthy track record of
following through on what I say I will do. It takes time to develop credibility, but it's much easier to lead when people
trust you. Very recently, I received a text from a friend who is
serving at a new church. He wanted my advice on how to deal
with a problem that arose on his second Sunday in the pulpit.
It was an issue of trust. Because he is new, someone in the
church is hesitant to trust what he says. And until trust has

time to be built in that context, he may deal with similar short-term issues.

For many of us, the Lord is someone we're just meeting. The rest of us may have known Him for years and even decades, yet the pressures we face in this world sometimes test the depth of our faith and trust. Knowing this to be the case, the writer of the book of Hebrews encourages us to "hold fast the confession of our hope without wavering" (10:23). I'm sure this writer had seen the hope of many people waver during the seasons of intense persecution that were endured during that period. Admittedly, it can be challenging to trust God and believe His promises when we feel pressed or threatened from every side, but that's precisely what the author of Hebrews tells us to do.

Why should we trust the Lord's promises?

Why shouldn't we give up hope?

The writer of Hebrews answers those questions for us and tells us that "he who promised is faithful" (verse 23). God is faithful to deliver on every assurance He has made. It would be inconsistent with His holy character for Him to lie. In fact, it's impossible for Him to lie. He is perfect truth. He is perfect light. In Him there is no deception or dishonesty. He is worthy of our respect because He always follows through on what He says He will do.

When we choose not to believe that the Lord will keep His promises to us, we find ourselves without a viable alternative. Most people, if they doubt the validity of God's promises, turn to some form of humanism. They trade the promises of God for the philosophies of man. And when they do that, their faith becomes tethered to fickle foundations that will eventually shift and crumble.

There may be people from your childhood who failed to keep the promises they made to you. There may be people in your family, at your work, or even in your church who have let you down as well. But God is faithful and will keep every promise He has made to you.

If you tell yourself that God keeps His promises, your outlook will change.

If you trust that the Lord will keep His assurances, you'll experience greater rest.

If you believe that the Lord always keeps His word, you will be more likely to internalize the teaching of His Word and less likely to adopt the foundationless philosophies of humanism as your own.

DWELL ON THIS

Today I will remember that even though this world is filled with people who give false assurances and break pledges, the Lord will never fail to keep His promises to me.

Today is a great day to display the gentleness of Christ.

Remind them to be submissive to
rulers and authorities, to be
obedient, to be ready for every
good work, to speak evil of no one,
to avoid quarreling, to be gentle,
and to show perfect courtesy
toward all people.

—Titus 3:1–2

When I was a child, I loved snow. As I grew older, my feelings toward it became mixed. I enjoyed skiing on it, but I didn't care for shoveling it.

Early in my years as a pastor, I served at a church whose building was on a corner. Its location offered great visibility, but a corner lot also meant that it had an extensive sidewalk. Most of the time that's fine, but when a hefty snowstorm drops many inches of wet snow and you don't own a snowblower, a sidewalk that long looks daunting.

I remember asking the church board when I first moved there, "What systems do we have in place for snow removal?"

I was told, "The funeral director owns a plow, so we pay him to handle the parking lot, but we expect the pastor to clear the sidewalks." Because I didn't want to seem like an entitled wimp with an office job, I didn't complain. But there seemed to be one glaring issue with that plan: What would we do if it snowed on a Sunday?

I don't know if this is technically accurate, but it seems to me as if most of the significant winter storms in Pennsylvania show up on weekends. True to form, one February weekend, a big storm arrived on a Saturday night. It left more than a foot of heavy, wet snow to clean up the next morning before services. Knowing that people were going to start arriving around nine thirty, I got to work clearing the sidewalks around six. I was optimistic that would give me enough time to remove the snow and also allow me to get cleaned up and ready to lead the worship service.

It took hours to shovel. By the time I was done, the snow was piled about four feet high around the edge of the property. I was exhausted, but thankfully my shovel didn't break. My back, on the other hand, felt as if it were going to spend the rest of that week in pain. I rushed back home, cleaned up, then ran back over to the church to greet people.

As I held the door and shook hands, a car pulled up and a woman opened her door to exit near the path I'd dug out earlier that gave her clear access to the sidewalk. When she stepped out of the car, she placed her foot in some slush. It wasn't much, but apparently it was enough to set her off. She looked up and yelled, "Who is responsible for cleaning these sidewalks? This is unacceptable!"

In that moment, I was exhausted. I had just spent hours shoveling without assistance and still had many hours of ministry ahead of me that day. For the most part, I was happy to serve the church by shoveling, but her response was not what I was expecting. I had thought someone might express appreciation for the work I had done, but instead my labor was harshly criticized.

I have to admit that her insensitive response felt insulting and instigated feelings of anger within me. But by God's grace, I didn't outwardly react. I held the door for her, welcomed her, and carried on with my responsibilities. My body was in pain. I felt tired and hungry. My efforts were unappreciated, but I didn't want to make the situation worse by overreacting. Christ has shown gentleness to me, and I believe He wants me to model His gentleness to others.

However, it's easier to be gentle when you aren't being tested. When I'm holding a newborn or moving a delicate piece of glassware, I'm instinctively gentle in order to prevent injury or damage. But newborns and glassware don't insult me. They aren't harsh or severe. They are powerless to do anything to prevent being hurt. All they can do is trust that they will be handled with care.

Grown adults are a different story. Sometimes they hurt those who help them, criticize those who attempt to encourage them, and harm those who love them. If you've ever served in a helping profession, you've probably experienced this too. Anytime we attempt to come alongside hurting people, we run the risk of being hurt ourselves.

I appreciate the advice Titus received in the New Testament letter that bears his name. He was serving as pastor among people who had a reputation for being harsh, but he was advised by Paul not to adopt that behavior as his own. He was encouraged to model a new standard that was based on the heart of Christ. Paul told Titus not to speak evil of people, to avoid quarreling, to be gentle, and to be courteous toward others (Titus 3:2). This counsel wasn't selective. Titus was told to display these traits "toward all people," not just toward those who were gentle with him.

This is a lesson I'm still trying to learn, as I frequently forget that I was a mess when Christ first stepped into my life. Because I was young, I find it easy to dismiss that season as a forgivable time of immaturity, but selective forgetfulness would be a mistake. Christ did a miracle in my life, and I want to spend the new life He's granted me remembering to display my gratefulness for His intervention.

When Christ found me, I was foolish, disobedient, ungrateful, unwise, and enslaved to worldly values and ambitions. Because that was a long time ago, it's easy for me to forget how ungrateful I was for everything He did on my behalf. It's easy for me to forget about the fact that, up to that point, I wasn't thanking Him for the pain He endured to serve me. For the most part, all I was doing during that season of life was complaining about how I wanted to be served in additional ways.

Jesus would have been perfectly justified in telling me to bug off, but that isn't what He did. He showed me kindness before I started noticing what He was doing. Then He remained gentle with me once I started growing in my young faith. Even now, He continues to display His gentleness in my life, even though I frequently make errors and act in ignorance. As I mature, He's teaching me to value His gentleness more and more. He's even giving me examples I can learn from as I observe the people He's placed in my life. One of those examples is the chancellor of the university where I teach.

Before I was an adjunct professor, I was a student, and the chancellor was the university president at that time. When I was fresh out of high school, we got to know each other a little. I'm particularly glad he allowed me to remain a student at his school even after he got to know me.

In college I was blessed with several roommates who shared my twisted sense of humor. For the most part, we were good students, but now and then our attempts to make each other laugh or gross each other out would cross the line.

During the homecoming weekend of our junior year, my friend Jeremy tried his hand at a carnival game for which goldfish were the prizes. He won several fish, but they quickly died. A normal person might have flushed them down the toilet, but Jeremy decided it would be more entertaining to stuff them in my on-campus mailbox. When I found them, I was repulsed and not very happy that the smell of dead fish was likely to cling to my papers and mail for a few weeks until that box aired out.

I wasn't sure how I was going to respond, but a few hours later I had a flash of inspiration. As I was driving back to campus after a quick visit to the store with our roommate Paul, a squirrel ran in front of my car. Thankfully, I missed it, but there was another squirrel running after the first one, and that one ran right under the tires of my car. We were driving on a side street when it happened, so it was safe for Paul and me to get out and look at the carnage. For the most part, the squirrel was intact, so I pushed it to the side of the road with a stick, then got back in the car.

I'm sure you see where this story is going. It didn't take long for Paul and me to get the bright idea to stuff that dead squirrel in Jeremy's mailbox. We grabbed a bag, turned the car around, picked up that squirrel carcass, and brought it back to campus with us.

At the time, the student mailboxes consisted of a large wall of locked cubbies that didn't reach all the way to the ceiling. There was just enough space at the top of that wall for a person to climb over and access the other side (if he or she were ambitious). Being rather ambitious, I chose to do just that when no one was around to see me. I took the bagged squirrel, climbed over the boxes, and stuffed its bloated dead body in Jeremy's mailbox. He found it the next day and was thoroughly disgusted.

I assumed that the joke would end there, but it didn't. In fact, when the school administration caught wind of what had happened, they restricted all access to the student boxes. No mail could be delivered and no papers would be returned until the administration figured out what was going on and who was behind the prank. The mail issue became a huge problem on campus and a major inconvenience to students and professors alike.

Paul and I knew we had to confess. We made an appointment with the dean of students. She was shocked that we were the culprits, as we both were elected officers in student government. She said, "I never would have assumed it was the two of you, but the directive to shut down access to the mail came from the president. I'm sorry, but you're going to have to speak with him."

I couldn't believe how big of an issue this was becoming, and Paul and I had no idea how the president was going to respond, but we made an appointment to meet with him and make our confession. When he opened the door to his office, he invited us in, and we told him what we had done. He could have been abrasive and severe in his response, but he chose another route. He said, "Gentlemen, what you did is more serious than you realize. Not only is it unsafe to scale that wall of mailboxes, but it's also illegal. That's federally protected property. Next time, if you want to give your friend a squirrel, mail it to him in a box or stuff it in his pillow, but don't tamper with campus mail. Have a good day."

We sat there for a moment in shock. Was he actually going to let us off this gently? We couldn't believe his kindness, but we were grateful. As an added bonus, every time I saw the president of our university for the rest of my time as a student, he smirked and said, "Hello, John." I always appreciated that he knew my name, and I couldn't help being amused by the fact that whenever he saw me, he was probably thinking about that dead squirrel being stuffed in a mailbox.

Jesus has been gentle to each of us on an even bigger scale than the college president was to me, so today would be a great time for us to show gentleness to others. Maybe they won't appreciate it, or maybe they will and, for the rest of their lives, they'll tell the story of the Christlike gentleness they were shown one day in college.

DWELL ON THIS

As a grateful recipient of Christ's gentleness, I will display the gentleness of Christ to someone else today.

Be respectful, even if you disagree.

Who is there to harm you if you are zealous for what is good? But even if you should suffer for righteousness' sake, you will be blessed. Have no fear of them, nor be troubled, but in your hearts honor Christ the Lord as holy, always being prepared to make a defense to anyone who asks you for a reason for the hope that is in you; yet do it with gentleness and respect, having a good conscience, so that, when you are slandered, those who revile your good behavior in Christ may be put to shame. For it is better to suffer for doing good, if that should be God's will, than for doing evil.

—1 Peter 3:13–17

Have you ever tried to tell people something they need to know, only to discover they have zero interest in listening? I have experienced this phenomenon more times than I care to count. I can think of multiple conversations with friends and family that have followed this pattern. I have also encountered this issue when speaking in a church, counseling in an office, and teaching in a classroom. Disregard is a common human response to unwanted and unsought information. It's frequently the way people initially respond to the gospel as well—a lesson I learned in college.

As a freshman, I was very excited to experience campus life. I went to a Christian college that emphasized the Bible in the curriculum, campus culture, and student life. It was a refreshing environment to live in as a student, and I didn't take it for granted. I was grateful to be surrounded by friends and professors who loved Jesus as much as I did and who had a burning desire to tell others about Him.

One afternoon, a group of us were sitting around on the floor of my friend's dorm room, chatting about issues related to life and faith. Most of us were big music fans, and one of the guys (Mike) brought up that the Grateful Dead were going to be playing in Philly that night. He said, "Wherever they play, large groups of people show up and hang out in the parking lot. They don't even go into the show. They just stay there, hanging out, drinking, and getting high. What would you guys think about walking around the parking lot telling people about Jesus?"

I liked Mike's idea, and others did too, so we loaded up several cars and drove to the parking lot of the Philadelphia Spectrum. We didn't have much of a plan other than to walk around, engage people in conversation, and share the gospel.

I had no idea what to expect. I didn't know if people would respond favorably, ambivalently, or with hostility.

When we got to the parking lot and started walking around, I was surprised to see how many people were outside the show with no plans to go inside. Groups of people gathered around cars, sat in circles, stood and laughed, or lay on the ground unconscious. I wasn't surprised to see quite a few people smoking pot, but something else caught my attention: it seemed that many of the groups were passing around balloons and inhaling whatever was inside them. I asked a friend, "Any idea what that's about?" He said, "They're getting high off nitrous oxide. It's laughing gas." Moments later, a generous guy about my age offered me a puff. I graciously declined. He shrugged his shoulders as if to say, "Your loss."

A few minutes later, we sat down with a group of people who looked to be about our age and started asking them questions. We discovered that one of the girls was from the town of Wilkes-Barre, where my mother grew up, so we chatted with her for a while. She seemed open to talking about spiritual subjects and what it means to have genuine faith in God. It was a pleasant conversation. I noticed she was also selling bumper stickers that said, "Mean People Suck," so I supported her entrepreneurial endeavors and bought two.

During our time there, we had a few additional conversations with people, most of which were rather uneventful and unmemorable. As we walked back to our cars, we encountered a man who gave us the impression he was homeless. He was sitting on a bench, holding multiple plastic bags in his left hand. We stood across from him and shared a little about faith, but he took offense at our words. He became angry and combative and started making a scene. Instead of conversing with us, he yelled. We didn't yell back but instead tried to share more about the ways God can change lives. That didn't interest him, so he increased his volume more and started screaming, "Will your God put food in my stomach?" He said it over and over—not in a desperate tone, but with a spirit of mockery. In fact, he smiled when he could tell he was making us uncomfortable.

Within moments, hundreds of people circled around us to watch what was taking place. Some were high. Some were drunk. Some were sober. The man was yelling at the three of us who were standing there together, and I wasn't sure what kind of response the crowd was going to have to this commotion. As the guy continued yelling, a man from the crowd walked up to him with a bottle of wine, sat down next to him, took a sip, and offered him a sip as well. Then they both joined together in yelling. We tried to respond to their comments in a way that seemed logical to us, but they didn't want to listen. It was clear that a productive conversation wasn't going to happen in this context, so we thanked them, excused ourselves, and walked away disappointed. We had something valuable to share, but we didn't get to share it. We weren't even sure if the approach we had taken to share the gospel was effective. I mean, we knew we were right in our beliefs, but we didn't seem to convince anyone else of it that night.

Have you ever noticed how destructive the desire to prove you're right can be? How many conversations have you experienced in your life that involved very little listening because both parties were more concerned with proving their points? Can a verbal exchange even be called a conversation if listening isn't an integral part of it?

What about prayer? Are your prayers even remotely conversational? Do you give time for God to speak? Do you wait for His answer, or do you spend the majority of your time trying to persuade Him of the righteousness of your requests?

Have you ever made the mistake of watching the interchanges that take place on political talk shows? Does anyone find that kind of speaking persuasive? I don't think my mind has ever been changed by the put-downs, insults, and talking over one another that take place on those programs. The only thing I think I've ever changed after attempting to watch is the channel.

I'm grateful and amazed that Jesus is even willing to associate with us. Sometimes it feels as though we're more prone to embarrass Him than glorify Him, yet Scripture tells us that Jesus is pleased to make us His ambassadors. We represent Him to a lost world, and He allows us to speak on His behalf. In fact, He's often speaking through us to many people who would prefer to mock and yell more than they would like to listen. But is there a way He would prefer us to speak? Is there an approach that might be more fruitful when we're trying to communicate the truth that's changed our lives?

In 1 Peter 3:15, Peter gives us some powerful counsel that was modeled for him by Jesus and impressed upon his heart by the Holy Spirit. Following the example of Christ, Peter advised us to be prepared to give others specific reasons for the hope that lives within us. He seemed to be indicating that there are going to be unexpected opportunities that will come our way when others express curiosity about what makes us tick.

You may encounter a hurting friend who is searching for hope in the midst of a seemingly hopeless season of life.

You may stand before an authority who offers you the chance to make a public defense of your faith.

You may be talking with a depressed teenager who can't see beyond his or her discouragement or insecurity.

You may encounter a screaming man who has lived a difficult life and finds it hard to believe God could be compassionate enough to fill his belly *and* his soul.

Be prepared to share the hope of Jesus with them. Answer them when they inquire about the hope your life is anchored to. Give them a taste of true hope by letting them see the light in your eyes and hear the joy in your voice. Prepare for these moments by learning to listen to God when He's speaking to you in prayer, in His Word, and through His people. And when you share about your hope in Christ, don't be arrogant or all-knowing. Show humility. Answer gently. Offer respect, even if it isn't reciprocated.

One of the greatest traits of Jesus that we celebrate when we read about His ministry was His ability to show honor and respect to people who weren't used to receiving it. When children wanted to get near Him, He welcomed them and didn't make them feel stupid for invading His personal bubble. He didn't demean people who had contagious skin diseases and open sores. He wasn't embarrassed to share a meal with convicted crooks or people with bad reputations. He even comforted the thief who was crucified next to Him by assuring him that he would be joining Him that very day in paradise.

Jesus won my heart, and He didn't win it by degrading me. He didn't win it by ignoring me when I spoke. He didn't win it by making me feel stupid, unsought, or unwanted. Rather, His words and actions convinced me that He valued me, heard me, and specifically wanted me to be with Him forever.

If I could go back to the parking lot of the Spectrum that night in October 1994, I would do some things exactly the same way, and some things drastically differently. I would once again sit down with the girl from Wilkes-Barre, listen to her thoughts about God, share some of my thoughts with her, and buy a few more bumper stickers. Then I would go over to the homeless man, treat him to a soft pretzel from one of the vendors, engage him in conversation while sitting next to him (instead of standing in front of him), listen to his story if he were willing to tell it, then respectfully share the reason for my hope in Jesus Christ. I think those methods could have contributed to a much better outcome.

Life isn't about proving you're right. It isn't about coming out on top of every debate. Christ's ministry and Peter's teaching both demonstrate to us that we will win more arguments by showing respect. If we want to earn the opportunity to share our hope, we need to walk in the steps Jesus marked out for us.

Tell yourself that every conversation isn't a court case.

Tell yourself that you'll never change a mind through arrogance.

Tell yourself that only Christ can change a heart, so give those you speak with a glimpse of your changed heart by showing them some Christ-centered respect.

DWELL ON THIS

Today I will be respectful, even if I disagree with someone. Being respectful will open more doors to sharing my hope in Christ than arrogance ever could.

DAY 18

Unhealthy habits and desires don't need to control you.

I remind you to fan into flame the gift of God, which is in you through the laying on of my hands, for God gave us a spirit not of fear but of power and love and self-control.

—2 Timothy 1:6–7

I live five minutes from almost everything. Literally. You can bring up whatever "something" you want, and I'm pretty sure I can be there within three hundred seconds.

The grocery store is five minutes away. The coffee shop is as well. Within five minutes, I can be at Home Depot, Walmart, a gas station, a train station, a river, a lake, or a beautiful park. Within a five-minute-drive from my front door are two malls, two movies theaters, and two Chick-fil-A restaurants. I didn't realize that fact when I bought my house, but since moving here, I have been amazed at how quickly I can drive to nearly everything I want or need.

That can be both good and bad, as my doctor recently confirmed.

I stopped by my doctor's office a couple of months ago to
get my annual checkup. He asked me a few questions, looked
at my eyes and ears, and tested my reflexes. Then he sent me
to get some blood work done. When the results came back a
few days later, I learned that my cholesterol is elevated. That
wasn't what I wanted to hear, but I'd be lying if I said it surprised me. I don't think I'm being careful enough with what
I eat, especially when I'm stressed out.

I lead a rather active and stressful life. There are quite a few
things under my oversight. I have family responsibilities, the
daily demands of ministry, and a mission board that I oversee.
At all hours of the day, I'm receiving calls, texts, and emails
that contain genuine problems and sometimes needless
drama. Most of the time, I think I handle all this well. But on
occasion, I try to medicate my stress.

People deal with stress in different ways. Many of our attempts are unhealthy and unwise. I don't drink alcohol, and I
don't do drugs. My unhealthy stress medication is high-
cholesterol foods. I think I love them all. I love fried chicken
in all its forms and interpretations, french fries, potato chips,
and funnel cake. I love ice cream, cheese, onion rings, and
snack cakes too. Sometimes I think that the only reason I go to
the gym is so I can loosely justify eating these things as regularly as I do.

It's challenging for me to resist these delicious foods because I can access them all within five short minutes. And in
my quest to medicate my stress, I have frequently made the
drive to Chick-fil-A for their delicious sandwiches or to Panda
Express for their perfectly fried orange chicken.

But then, after enjoying such delicious items, I made the

mistake of going to my doctor and letting him and his wicked team of phlebotomists ruin the fun. The nerve.

I'm glad they ruined the fun for me. I'd like to stick around for a little while, and I'm jeopardizing my chances of longevity if I allow my unhealthy passion for high-cholesterol foods to control me.

There's an interesting verse in the book of Philippians that seems to invite questioning looks when I speak on it from time to time. In Philippians 3:19, it says, "Their end is destruction, their god is their belly, and they glory in their shame, with minds set on earthly things." That verse is referencing those who live as "enemies of the cross of Christ" (verse 18).

Did you notice who that verse says the enemies of Christ worship? Scripture states that "their god is their belly" (emphasis added). That's certainly an interesting way to describe someone who rejects Jesus and actively works against the proclamation of His gospel.

Paul was expressing that the people he was describing worshipped their fleshly appetites. They lived and died to try to satisfy the cravings of their sinful natures. In essence, their bellies were their masters because their cravings held ultimate sway over their lives.

Joking about our bellies is easier than taking care of them. Recently, one of my sons volunteered some of his time to help an area ministry. One of the tasks they asked him to assist with was printing T-shirts that could be given to the people they were ministering to. After being taught how to do that, he said to me, "Hey, Dad, would you like a T-shirt too? I can basically print whatever you'd like on it." I thought about his offer for a few seconds and said, "Absolutely. Make me a shirt with six-pack abs printed on it. That's certainly easier than eating right." He replied, "Believe it or not, I knew that's exactly what you were going to say."

All kidding aside, I don't want my belly to be my god. I already have a God who loves me and wants more for me than I want for myself. And I'm certain that He doesn't want me to be controlled by unhealthy appetites and passions of any kind.

Have you ever tried to identify some of the unhealthy passions that are trying to control you? Is there a god of your belly that wants you to make sacrifices of your time, health, and finances? You do realize that if you know Christ, you don't need to cede control of yourself to your old appetites any longer, right?

Second Timothy 1:7 tells us, "God gave us a spirit not of fear but of power and love and self-control." At the moment we come to faith in Jesus, we are radically transformed. The Holy Spirit takes residence within us and empowers us with His divine strength. As a result, we no longer need to walk in fear, we no longer need to rely on our limited strength, we no longer need to be consumed by hatred, and we don't have to yield control of our lives to anyone other than the Lord.

Being that we're empowered by the presence of the Spirit, we can practice self-discipline and self-control. He grants us the privilege and ability to demonstrate these traits. He also gives us the desire to want what He wants for our lives. Because God values order, He enables us to value what He values: control, not chaos; discipline, not self-destruction.

However, unhealthy passions are a power force to be reckoned with. It would be unwise of me to pretend that the battle isn't challenging. It can be very difficult to give up our unhealthy passions when we've depended on them for so long to medicate our pain.

Willpower alone often isn't enough to make changes. I witnessed a clear example of this several months ago when I was called to the hospital to pray with a grieving family. Their twenty-two-year-old son lay on a bed, unconscious, and they had just been told he didn't have much time left. The doctors did everything they could for him, but it appeared that his body was shutting down and wouldn't recover.

The young man had overdosed on a blend of illegal drugs that was frequently fatal. Sadly, it wasn't the first time he had done that. His appetite for feeding his drug addiction was so strong that he regularly gave in to it, even after promising his friends, family, therapists, and doctors that he would quit. At one point in the conversation, the young man's mother said, "I don't know what else to do for him. If the Lord decides to take him, I need to have peace with that decision. This isn't something I can fix for him, and nothing he tries seems to break his cycle of addiction."

I told her, "I can't imagine the grief you're enduring, but since we don't know the particulars of what God has in store for your son, let's pray with the hope that God will resuscitate him and bring him ultimate healing." She agreed and we stood near his bed to pray.

Prior to driving to the hospital, I had asked our church family to pray for this young man, so I knew that while we prayed around his bed, there were many other people praying for him as well. Even though the doctors hadn't offered much hope for the recovery of this young man, we trusted that the Lord could do something miraculous.

Together we prayed in faith. Several days later, the young man regained consciousness. Since that time, he's been receiving additional treatment and guidance. God gave a miraculous response to our prayers.

Often when I witness a situation like that, I wish we could

go back in time to a day before this young man decided to try his first drug. I would love to be able to have an honest conversation with him about what's causing him pain and discouragement. I'd love to have the opportunity to help him see that we're all in the midst of a battle with the god of our stomachs and that we all have mistakenly believed that giving in to their appetites would ease our pain. But feeding the god of our bellies doesn't reduce pain; it creates more pain—for ourselves and for those who love us.

You don't need to be mastered by your flesh. You don't need to be dominated by your old nature. You don't need to make additional sacrifices to satisfy the destructive demands of your former god.

If you are in Christ, let Him direct your steps. Let the Spirit shape your appetite.

DWELL ON THIS

> Today is a good day to tell myself that my unhealthy passions don't need to control me any longer. Christ is Lord over my appetites and passions.

Don't adopt this world's depressive outlook as your own.

Do not be conformed to this world,
but be transformed by the renewal
of your mind, that by testing you
may discern what is the will of
God, what is good and acceptable
and perfect.

—*Romans* 12:2

Have you ever received a hug that mattered to you in the moment but matters even more to you now? My grandmother's hug was just that.

My father's mother was one of the loveliest people I've been blessed to know. We called her Grammie, and when I was little, she watched my sisters and me every Wednesday. It was my favorite day of the week. She would take us for walks on the quiet, tree-lined streets of her neighborhood. We would collect acorns and leaves and chat with many of the friendly neighbors who lived near her. Then we'd go back to her house for lunch. I would ask her to put mayo and mustard on my sandwiches, which at first she thought was weird but accommodated my request anyway. One day, out of curiosity, she gave it a try and liked it so much she started eating her sandwiches that way too.

It wasn't just my taste in food that Grammie wanted to experience for herself. From a very young age, I was an avid music listener. On occasion, Grammie would borrow some of my albums to check out what I was into at the time. This even happened during the "metal" phase of my early teenage years. Surprisingly, she actually enjoyed some of the bands. I doubt she would have discovered a liking to those things on her own, but she wanted to experience what I liked because she was making intentional attempts to connect with me.

Not only was Grammie interested in continually learning, but she was also a dispenser of wisdom. She once told me, "When you're listening to your music, pay attention to the words. The artist is trying to tell you a story." I took her counsel and made a point to do that. Later on she told me that was advice she had received from her father.

In general, Grammie was a good listener, not only to song lyrics but also to conversations and life concerns. If something mattered to me, it mattered to her. If something concerned me, it concerned her. This was a pattern I observed in her for the decades I was privileged to know her.

One afternoon, right after I turned thirty, I stopped by Grammie's house for a quick visit. She had recently been diagnosed with lung cancer, but the doctors believed they might be able to extend her otherwise healthy life if they removed the lung that was affected. She was heading to the hospital the next day, so I dropped by to chat with her and pray for God's help and intervention.

After I prayed, Grammie gave me a hug. She always hugged me when I visited, but this time she held on. There was more emotion behind that hug than normal, and I could clearly sense it. When she relaxed her squeeze, she stepped back and looked at me. Her eyes were glassy with tears and she said, "Well, I guess there's nothing left for me to do than to trust whatever God decides. If He lets me stick around here for a while, I'll be grateful, but if it's my time to go, I'm ready to go. I'm content either way."

The next day, she had her surgery. Everything went well and the doctors told us what we could expect with Grammie's recovery process. Later that day, I talked to her on the phone and she sounded really strong. But the following day, something changed. Her body rapidly started shutting down, and it became clear to the medical staff that she wasn't going to make it. Our family rushed to the hospital and surrounded her bed. We held her hands, prayed with her, and said our goodbyes.

The hardest goodbye to watch was from my grandfather. When the nurses told us she was nearly gone, my grandfather put his head close to Grammie's and whispered something in her left ear. None of us knows what he said, but she lifted both her arms into the air. From where I stood at the foot of her bed, it looked like she was reaching for one more hug. My grandfather kissed her cheek and hugged her head close to his, and moments later she passed.

When I had visited Grammie a couple days earlier, I couldn't have known that I was receiving the last hug I would from Grammie. I enjoyed it in the moment, but in retrospect, I'm truly grateful that she held on a little longer than normal. Her affection created a memory that remains locked in my brain.

Her words are forever with me as well. There was so much wisdom she expressed to me while I was growing up, but when she was facing possible death, she made a point to share one of the most important. She showed me how it looks to trust God in the midst of fear. As she contemplated her future, she did so with hope. She was content in the Lord and trusted that whatever outcome He ordained for her situation would be the right one.

How deep is our trust in the Lord's sovereignty over the outcome of our lives? What perspective do we gravitate toward when we contemplate the future?

This world doesn't share the same perspective we're blessed with as believers in Christ. Through Him, we've been given a new mind, which is a wonderful gift. The gift of a renewed mind means we don't need to adopt this world's depressive outlook as our own. We can face trials with hope, and fearful moments with faith.

Admittedly, however, this world still has influence over us if we let it. When we're surrounded by scores of people who have adopted grim views toward the future, it can be easy to adopt those perspectives as our own. And though it can be easy for us to conform to the manner of thinking we're observing in others, God has made it possible for us to avoid this trap.

Nearly every day, I hear stories of worry: worry about the future of this earth, worry about the future of our nation, worry about the dips and dives of our economy, worry about the health of humanity. And when I hear these stories, it can be easy for me to gradually conform to the troubling outlook. Though it's not pleasant or uplifting, that negative view does a good job of rooting itself into my thought life more than it should.

This outlook is nothing new. We see examples of it during the days of the early church as well. When Paul wrote his letter to the church in Rome (which became the book of Romans), he was writing to people who lived in a culture that was opposed to the mindset of Christ. It was a culture that celebrated vice and coveted power. It was a culture that worshipped mythical deities who promised to feed the cravings of the flesh—a culture that was known for its brutality and blood lust.

These early Christians were surrounded by people, structures, and belief systems that fed an ungodly and bleak outlook, but we're surrounded by the very same things. The scale and emphasis may differ, but the substance and root issues remain the same.

The pressure to conform is one of the strongest pressures we experience. The way we dress, style our hair, raise our children, and speak our language reveals our level of conformity. The way we use our time and spend our money also demonstrates our conformity level. Just the other day, I was chided by a friend because he thinks I should use credit cards so I can earn rewards and points when I spend. I told him, "I think I spend more when I buy things on credit, so I'm going to stick with my debit card and cash." He told me I was missing out and shook his head in pity.

When Christ redeems us, He sends us into the world to represent Him, not to conform to the gloomy mentality He rescued us from. Through His Spirit, He is transforming us. He is renewing our minds and enabling us to see life from His perspective. If we embrace the renewal He is accomplishing within us, we will begin to perceive things that once escaped our attention.

Frequently, I'm asked, "How can I know God's will for my life?" I suspect that's something most of us have wrestled with. It's a good question, but there's a distinct reason many people struggle to find an answer. If we spend decades conforming to this world, that means we're also becoming adept at squelching our conscience and ignoring God's voice.

How can we possibly expect to know God's will if we refuse to listen when He speaks?

In Romans 12:2, Paul said, "Be transformed by the renewal of your mind, that by testing you may discern what is the will of God." If we want to understand God's will for us, we can't continue to embrace our old way of thinking. We can't continue to adopt this world's depressive outlook as our own. We need to adopt a pattern of renewed thinking that's the fruit of listening to God's voice instead of ignoring Him.

When I was a child, I thought about what the Lord had in store for me. I gradually came to believe that His plan was good and perfect. My life has taken a few unexpected turns, and I've experienced my share of painful trials, but my outlook remains hopeful. My tribulations don't entrap my hope. My momentary pain doesn't rob me of the joy I have in Christ. I'm learning to see all things with His eyes as He renews my mind and frees me from unhealthy conformity.

Are you still conforming your thought life and your outlook to this world's dismal patterns?

Can you see beyond your momentary circumstances into the hope God offers you?

Are you ignoring God's voice, or listening to Him?

Can you discern God's will for you?

You learn a lot about a person's faith when it's being tested. My grandmother realized there was a distinct possibility she was living her last days on this earth. In those moments, she didn't curse her trials or shake her fists at God. She hugged her family, and then with the last ounce of strength she had left, she reached out her arms to the Lord. He embraced her and took her to be with Him always.

DWELL ON THIS

Today I will remind myself that I won't hold tightly to this world. It won't hug me back. I won't adopt its depressive outlook. I will extend my arms to Christ and welcome His embrace. He has good and perfect things in store for me.

DAY 20

The Lord hears your cry for mercy.

I love the LORD, because he has
    heard
  my voice and my pleas for
    mercy.
Because he inclined his ear to me,
  therefore I will call on him as
    long as I live.

           —Psalm 116:1–2

My weekly schedule tends to be the direct opposite of most people's. The most common schedules seem to involve working from nine to five, Monday through Friday, with evenings, weekends, and holidays off. But that schedule could never work for a pastor. I have ministry commitments many evenings. Our primary worship services are on Sunday, and most holidays require extra time and effort, not rest. One perk of my schedule, however, is that I can usually take Mondays off. I'm almost always exhausted on Mondays, so that suits me just fine.

But not every Monday is a day of rest. Sometimes I have responsibilities that require me to stop by my office. A few years ago, on a hot summer day right after the Fourth of July, I had a Monday like that. I didn't need to do much at the office and didn't plan to remain long, but I stopped by on my day off to take care of a few odds and ends.

Our church parking lot is behind our building. As I pulled into the driveway that runs along the edge of our property and prepared to park, I noticed something strange in the back of the lot. It looked as if something were creating a large plume of smoke behind a tree, but I couldn't discern what it was. I pulled my car a little closer to see if I could figure it out, and that's when I realized that the entire tree was on fire. Without giving it much more thought, I parked my car, ran into the church, and grabbed a fire extinguisher.

I always forget how messy extinguishers are, but let me assure you if you've never used one, they are. They're especially messy when a nice breeze is blowing in your direction. As I pulled the pin on the extinguisher and began spraying the tree, the wind made a point to blow a considerable amount of the fire retardant back on me. It was in my hair, on my clothing, and covering my shoes. This certainly wasn't my idea of a restful day off.

I sprayed the tree with as much powder as I could, but it wasn't effective. The extinguisher ran out, and it became clear to me that I would need to call the fire department. The fire had spread through parts of the tree that I couldn't even reach, and I was concerned that if I didn't get the blaze under control soon, it was going to begin spreading through the dry hillside and other trees in the vicinity. There's also a neighborhood home behind our property that I was highly concerned about.

It didn't take long for the fire department to arrive. I took some pictures of the tree, the trucks, the hoses, and the process of putting out the blaze. Thankfully, the firefighters were able to get the blaze under control before it spread and caused more damage. As we tried to figure out why the tree was on fire in the first place, we discovered a pile of used fireworks, which helped us piece the story together. Clearly, some kids had been messing with the explosives and lighting them off in our parking lot on a day when it didn't look like anyone was around.

The next day while I was in my office, I saw two kids outside near the edge of our parking lot, right where the blaze was burning the day before. They looked to be about middle school aged (when a fascination with fire is high on a boy's list of interests). They were snooping around the spot where I found the used fireworks, and it appeared they had brought a few more with them to light. I paused what I was doing and ran up to them. The tone of my voice, and the realization they had just been caught, clearly frightened them. I didn't know for absolute certain that these were the kids that had caused the fire, but I pretended to know in order to force a confession out of them.

I barked, "You're the kids who were here yesterday! Did you set this tree on fire accidentally, or was it on purpose?" They assured me it was an accident. Then I grabbed my phone and showed them the pictures I took the day before of the fire and the process it took to extinguish it. They looked mortified.

I explained to them the ramification of what they did, the danger it caused, and the cost that was paid to remedy it. By their expressions, I could tell they thought they were both in the biggest trouble they had ever been in. I'm guessing this was probably the worst mistake they had ever made, and I was probably still showing extra irritation over having been covered in the extinguisher powder, not to mention residual alarm from the potential devastation they could have caused.

With fear on his face, the taller boy said, "We're sorry." And I could tell he meant it.

At that point, I told them about a mistake my friend Aaron and I made when we were their age. We had been lighting little smoke bombs we'd bought at the pharmacy on a dry summer day and accidentally set fire to the baseball field behind our local high school. I was shocked at how fast the fire spread, but our local fire department responded quickly and took care of it.

I told those boys, "Look, I've been in your shoes. I know you're fascinated with fire, but you can't let something like this happen again. I'm not going to seek retribution against you or try to get you in trouble, but I'd like you to pick up the garbage you left behind yesterday and promise me this won't happen again." They were relieved and gratefully complied.

I don't know what you consider your worst mistake or act of rebellion to be, but I'm sure it isn't something you'd like to see someone else repeat. When I goof up, I tend to be harder on myself than anyone else is. I have made many mistakes in my life, some of which I openly talk about and others I prefer not to because they embarrass me.

But God knows every mistake I've ever made. He has seen my acts of rebellion, and His heart has grieved over each of them. When that boy looked me in the eye and said, "We're sorry," my heart was moved to show compassion. I have been on the receiving end of God's mercy more times than I realize, and that was a moment when I knew the Lord was asking me to show mercy to two scared kids who expected swift punishment for their crime.

Sometimes a cry for mercy sounds like, "We're sorry"; other times it just sounds like a whimper. But God hears both. We don't know who wrote Psalm 116, but whoever it was said, "I love the LORD, because he has heard my voice and my pleas for mercy" (verse 1).

Mercy is something we crave, but we're not always convinced we're going to receive it. I don't know what was going on in the psalmist's life when he first penned those words, but I have a few guesses as to what it could have been. Later in that psalm, he indicated that the Lord had rescued him from death. Could it maybe be that he was dealing with a disease and then the Lord mercifully healed him? Or was there a band of mercenaries searching for him in order to take his life? Whatever the case, it was clear to him that he needed divine intervention in order to survive the ordeal, and the Lord supplied precisely what he cried out to Him for.

How loud do you suppose you need to be for the Lord to hear you? Do you need to literally scream in order to grab His attention? Would you bother, or is your heart convinced that it wouldn't even make a difference? Could you whisper and get God's attention, or are you at the point when you've convinced yourself that your mistakes are too egregious for Him to show you His mercy at all?

The psalmist who composed Psalm 116 was convinced the Lord could hear him. He said, "[The Lord] inclined his ear to me" (verse 2). I picture an adult leaning down toward a child so that child can whisper "I'm sorry" in his ear. Can you envision God doing something like that for you? The psalmist could.

Good listeners are hard to come by. Most people like talking, but few demonstrate genuine interest in what someone else says. The psalmist experienced a powerful moment in his life when he became completely convinced that God is a good listener. God answered his plea for mercy. God heard his anguished voice. And having experienced the Lord's powerful response, the psalmist became confident in God. He said, "I will call on him as long as I live" (verse 2). God demonstrated that He listens to the pleas for mercy that His children bring before Him.

Making a plea for mercy isn't an easy thing to do. Before that plea is made, several things will most often have taken place. You will have had to admit to yourself that you have done something wrong or are experiencing something that's outside your control. You might have attempted to utilize your limited strength or the tools at your disposal to remedy the problem. You probably will have admitted that you are incapable of fixing whatever has been broken, and you'll start telling yourself that you're about to get the bad outcome you deserved in the first place.

But the story doesn't need to end there. In fact, God delights to show mercy to rebels who make the worst mistakes. By nature, He is the perfection of mercy, and when He sent Jesus Christ into this world, He intervened in human history with the greatest act of mercy imaginable: He gave His innocent, sinless Son to suffer wrath for us so we could become the eternal beneficiaries of mercy. Through faith in Christ, we become objects of God's mercy forever.

Why avoid calling out to God for mercy when He's already made you an object of it? Is your pride getting in the way of crying out to Him? Are you still trying to handle your dilemmas and anguish in your own strength? Have you forgotten how He sees you now that you've trusted in Jesus and accepted the work He accomplished on your behalf?

Mercy puzzles us because we know we don't deserve it. We

deserve judgment. We deserve to experience the effects of our bad decisions and poor planning. We deserve to pay for the messes we've made. The cost to extinguish the blaze we've ignited should come out of our pockets. But mercy tells a different story. With genuine mercy, God has chosen not to make us pay the cost of our offenses; His Son made the payment for us.

You need God's mercy, and you can cry out to Him for it. You don't have to be loud; you don't have to be soft; you just have to be genuine. I think that if He hears you and if you invite Him to respond to your need, He will convince you that He's always worth crying out to. He will make you realize that you can call on Him for as long as you live.

DWELL ON THIS

> Today I will remind myself that the Lord knows what I need, sees me in my moments of desperation, and hears my cries for mercy.

DAY **21**

Don't let fear of others hold you back from God's purpose for your life.

The LORD is my light and my
   salvation;
   whom shall I fear?
The LORD is the stronghold of my
   life;
   of whom shall I be afraid?

— *Psalm 27:1*

My mother was always faithful about taking our family to church on Sundays. Even when I gave her grief about it, she didn't budge. I didn't appreciate her insistence on doing this when I was a child, but as an adult, I regularly thanked her for it.

I was resistant to church during my early adolescence, but eventually I learned to love being part of our local church family. During my teen years, when it started to become clear to others that I was growing very serious about my faith in Christ, some of the leaders in our church decided to get me more plugged in to a variety of roles and responsibilities. They wanted to give me the opportunity to see what it's like to serve in local church ministry. I was fifteen at the time, and I happily agreed to every idea they suggested.

When they asked me to join the team of ushers and help collect the offering on Sunday mornings, I was glad to do so. It made me feel like one of the men of the church, which was a fraternity I definitely wanted to belong to. When they asked me to teach a preschool class during Vacation Bible School, I also agreed. I had no prior teaching experience, and I did a terrible job, but I learned a lot.

But then my pastor got the idea in his head that I should be reading Scripture from the pulpit on Sunday mornings. I was honored that he asked me but also slightly terrified. He would give me the verses ahead of time that he wanted me to read so I had the chance to become acquainted with them, but when Sunday morning came, I always felt physically sick. The thought of having to read in front of everyone filled me with fear. I was worried I would make a mistake and look foolish.

On the Sundays when I was asked to read, I would spend the first twenty minutes of the service shaking nervously in my pew, trying to function even though my stomach was in great pain. Then the pastor would call my name, and I would walk to the front of the church, climb the steps to the pulpit, and try to ignore the fact that everyone was looking at me. Then I would read the Scripture with a noticeably trembling voice. I was embarrassed by my own nervousness, but once I got through the experience, I would sit back down and allow myself to relax.

After doing this three or four Sundays, I asked my sister, "How did I do?" She said, "Well, you sounded really nervous, but the people here like you, so I'm sure they'll forgive you."

Her words weren't very comforting, and I think she realized that, but what she said was accurate.

Those nervous feelings continued throughout my teen and college years whenever I was asked to speak, which started to become a regular occurrence. I went from reading Scripture at our church to preaching sermons in various others. But each time I did so, I was terrified. I usually wouldn't sleep the night before, and the pain in my stomach would typically continue all morning until I was finished speaking.

It wasn't until the second or third year of being a full-time pastor that this pattern lessened. I knew the Lord had called me to serve as a pastor, and I understood the role required a considerable amount of public speaking, but because of the internal struggle taking place within me, it took quite a while for me to truly enjoy God's calling on my life.

What was at the root of my nervousness? What was causing the acids in my stomach to churn? As far as I can tell, the root cause of my trepidation was the fear of others. I was afraid of what others might say or what they might think about me after I finished speaking. I thought they would pick apart my content, criticize my delivery, and think less of me. But that's a terrible fear and certainly isn't the perspective the Lord wants any of us to adopt.

Life isn't about how I look. It isn't about my reputation or glory. I need to remain focused on giving Christ glory and helping people come to know Him in a deeper way. When I'm speaking, I need to be asking myself questions such as, *Am I honoring Jesus right now? Am I being faithful to sharing what this passage is teaching? Am I communicating something that will be helpful to those who carve out time to hear it?*

I have found that when my focus is on honoring Christ and

serving His people, my nervousness greatly subsides. In fact, even though I sometimes still feel slightly nervous before I speak to a group, I don't feel anything like I used to. Since I have taken the focus off me and turned it toward giving glory to Jesus by serving His people, my stomach has stopped swirling with pain in the hours before I speak and I manage to get some sleep the night before.

If I had let the fear of others become the dominant voice I allowed my heart to hear, I would have given up speaking a long time ago. Instead of embracing one of the main tasks the Lord has given me to do, I would have run from it. Thankfully, He has shifted my perspective and developed within me a genuine love for speaking, teaching, and leading. I look forward to the opportunities to do so, and I'm grateful the Lord allows me to do these things.

In Psalm 27:1, David contrasted the power of the Lord with the limited power of man. In the Lord, David found light. Through the Lord, he experienced salvation. In the midst of his experiences, David could see the powerful hand of God at work, which reminded him that he didn't need to be afraid of men. Yes, there would be people who stood against him. Yes, there would be people who opposed him or spoke poorly of him. But when he took a step back and considered the greatness of God, his inclination to remain fearful lessened. I like when he asked, "Of whom shall I be afraid?"

What has God called you to do with your life?

Whose criticism or opposition are you afraid of?

Are you allowing fear to hold you back from fulfilling the mission God has given you?

Sometimes it's our own irrational fear of others that holds us back. Other times, we actually encounter hurtful people who attempt to hold us down and hurt us.

Several times in my life, I have come across people who were highly critical of me and intentionally attempted to hold me back from doing what God was calling me to do. They all seem to use the same playbook. Here's what I've noticed about their approach:

Play 1: *They patronize.* In this stage, they attempt to dismiss or laugh at whatever you're attempting to do. They will try to make you feel small or make your idea sound impossible.

Play 2: *They demean.* If their patronization didn't convince you to quit, they will take it a step further and speak poorly of you and your plan in a more public way. They may even attempt to recruit several others to join them in opposing you.

Play 3: *They hurt.* If demeaning you wasn't enough to discourage your efforts, they may actively try to hurt you. They will take some sort of concrete step to inflict a more severe form of pain. Usually this comes in the form of emotional pain, but it frequently includes operational pain (through creating roadblocks that may slow you down) and, in more extreme situations, physical pain.

Play 4: *They defame.* If hurting you couldn't stop what you were called to do, they will covertly attack your reputation. Over time, you'll discover lies, half truths, and outright distortions that are being spread by those who have set themselves against you. Pay no mind to this. Don't get overly defensive. The Holy Spirit will fight this battle for you by revealing the truth (and your critics' motives) over time.

Play 5: *They hide.* When defaming you fails, your opposition will probably hide (at least for a while). They'll start to realize that their tactics aren't having the desired effect on you, and they'll probably move on while grumbling against you under their breath.

I have seen this pattern play out time and time again. It's

almost always exactly the same, just with a different cast of characters. Serving in a public role, I have become so familiar with this pattern that I practically chart it out in my mind when I witness it beginning to take place in my life or in the lives of other ministry leaders. Even though the opposition is unpleasant, the Lord reminds me that if my conscience is clear, I have nothing to fear. He is my stronghold, and there's no one I need to be afraid of.

With every major transition in my life, and in the midst of seasons of great blessing, I have had to deal with people who have tried to hold me back from God's purposes for my life. You may have experienced this as well. It's as if God opens doors, and then certain people feel the need to do everything they can to prevent you from walking through those doors. These people may try to get in your head, attack your family, question your motives, and hurt you in other ways, but the Lord has made it clear that you don't need to be afraid. He is your light. He is your salvation.

Would it be accurate for me to assume that the Lord has called and equipped you to do something you've hesitated to do because of your fear of others? Are you learning to trust Him in the midst of that fear, or are you still shrinking back from your calling because you're afraid of what other people might say or do?

The fear of man is a trap that prevents us from pursuing God's purpose for our lives. If we are governed by the fear of what others may say or do, we will ignore the voice of God as a result and very likely spend our lives inhibited by the low expectations and values of others. The following two verses provide comfort and encouragement for me, and I hope they will for you too:

The fear of man lays a snare,
     but whoever trusts in the LORD is safe.
          (Proverbs 29:25)

We can confidently say,

"The Lord is my helper;
     I will not fear;
          what can man do to me?" (Hebrews 13:6)

DWELL ON THIS

Starting today I will not allow the fear of others to hold me back. I will answer God's calling and embrace His promise to be my stronghold.

Pray for those who have intentionally hurt you.

Bless those who curse you, pray for
those who mistreat you.

—Luke 6:28, CSB

I don't spend much time being angry. For the most part, I think I'm becoming much quicker to overlook an offense than I once was, but as with all things, I still have room to grow. Every now and then, I'll experience something that will set me off and trigger an undesirable, angry response.

A few years back, I had an experience that really set me off. I was intentionally hurt by someone I have known for quite a few years. As juicy as it might be to share all the details, I'll refrain. What upset me isn't as important as what the Lord reminded me of in the midst of the experience.

For several months, I spent a portion of each day seething over the offense. My wife had to hear me complain about it repeatedly. My children knew plenty of the specifics as well. Come to think of it, everyone in my family knew about it, and amazingly, they all seemed to agree that I was the unfairly injured party. Somehow I managed to take that universal agreement as justification to stoke the fires of my anger even further.

This went on for a while, to the point that I was starting to enjoy my daily mental visits with my righteous indignation. It wasn't a healthy place to remain in, but because of the depth of the offense, I didn't rush to heal. I wanted to stew a little longer.

Finally, when it started to become clear to me that my anger was morphing into bitterness, I asked the Lord to intervene. I sought His help to change what I was feeling. I asked Him to liberate me from the anger over an offense that had been making my blood boil for many weeks. I'm grateful to be able to say that the Lord answered my prayer. He brought Luke 6:28 to my mind and reminded me to "pray for those who mistreat you" (CSB).

And that's exactly what I did. In the moments when I could feel my anger toward my offender bubbling up, I paused what I was doing and started to pray for him. After several days of that, I started praying for his family as well. I prayed that the Lord would bless them and grant them wisdom, strength, and protection. I asked the Lord to direct their steps and keep their hearts sensitive to His leading. In time, I could see evidence that the Lord was answering my prayers. And in the process, I also witnessed the healing of my heart.

When people hurt us, it isn't easy to move past the pain. It isn't easy to overlook the offense, particularly if they've hurt us in a major way.

I shared elements of this story one Sunday when I was preaching. As I spoke, I made the comment that in addition to praying for the man who had deeply offended me, I also followed up my prayers with action. I felt that the Lord was lead-

ing me to give that man a specific gift that had the potential
to bless his family in a meaningful way. The gift was well received and helped contribute toward further healing of our
fractured friendship. Just as Jesus said, "Bless those who curse
you," this was my attempt at heeding that counsel.

Afterward, two women asked if they could speak to me
before they left. They were good friends of each other. One
attended our church regularly, but the other was there for the
first time, having been invited by her friend.

With her friend's support, the visitor began sharing a story
with me. She told me about someone in her past who had hurt
her in many ways. She carried that pain around with her regularly and found it very difficult to move past. She even ac-
knowledged that the person who had hurt her probably didn't
spend any time thinking about the offense. To the other person
it was somewhat forgettable, but to her it was life changing.

The visitor said, "I really want to move past the pain I've
been harboring for a long time, so I appreciate your transpar-
ency this morning. I know I need to forgive the person who
hurt me, so I'm going to pray for him. And if I get the opportunity to bless him in a tangible way, I'm going to do that as
well." I was grateful to see the steps of faith this woman was
preparing to take that day.

Isn't it strange to observe how much time our minds can
spend dwelling on offenses? When people compliment us or
encourage us, we might feel good about their kindness for a
week or two, but then the emotion tends to fade. But when
people intentionally hurt us, we sometimes give them the opportunity to inflict a second blow by holding on to the offense for weeks, months, or years. They may have long
forgotten what they've done to us, but we think about it every
day while we grow bitter and sour.

The Lord hasn't called us to foster bitterness. When Jesus came to this earth, He came to people who had every intention of hurting Him. This didn't surprise Him. He knew He would be crucified at the hands of those who rejected Him. Yet even in the midst of the pain they were causing Him, Christ lifted them up in prayer to the Father.

When Christ calls us to pray for those who have intentionally hurt us, He isn't asking us to do something He wasn't willing to do Himself. He knows that it isn't easy. He knows we would much rather see vengeance come down upon our oppressors while we're angry. But anger, even anger that initially seems righteous, can harden into harmful bitterness if it isn't dealt with the right way. Christ calls us to respond with prayer—not only for the sake of the offending party but also for our sake, so that our lives won't be damaged by replaying the offenses over and over each day in our minds. He offers us the privilege to exchange retribution for grace, curses for blessing, and bitterness for joy:

> Let all bitterness and wrath and anger and clamor and slander be put away from you, along with all malice. Be kind to one another, tenderhearted, forgiving one another, as God in Christ forgave you. (Ephesians 4:31–32)

We're blessed to have the examples of many people who have come before us and shown us what it truly looks like to put Christ's teaching into practice. Praying for those who intentionally hurt us isn't easy to do, but it gets easier the further we are from the initial offense. But what if we could learn to pray for them while they're still inflicting the pain?

When I need some inspiration, I read the early chapters of the book of Acts, where we're given a picture of what life was like for Christians during the days right after Christ's resurrection and return to heaven. The men and women who are referenced in those chapters knew what it was like to have their faith tested, yet they continued to take steps of faith and risk their lives in order to help their unbelieving friends, family, and neighbors come to faith in Jesus as they had.

One of the examples of faith that stands out when reading Acts is a man named Stephen. Stephen had a reputation for being serious about his faith in Christ. He was devoted to the Lord and considered it a blessing to be able to serve others in Christ's name.

Stephen's faith wasn't a secret. It would have been impossible to know him during that era without realizing how committed he was to following Christ. We're also told that the Lord carried out miraculous signs and wonders through Stephen, which I'm sure was an attention-getter for believers and unbelievers alike. Eventually, those who hated Christ interrogated Stephen. This group included the high priest and others who considered themselves above average in religious devotion.

Acts 7 records Stephen's response to those men. As he spoke, he demonstrated his trust in Jesus while also pointing out that this group of men had historically rejected the voice of God when He attempted to intervene in their lives. The more Stephen spoke about Jesus, the angrier his interrogators became. When he had the audacity to point out that they were guilty of betraying and murdering Jesus, the men became incensed and prepared to also murder Stephen by stoning him.

What would you have done if you were in Stephen's place?

What would you have said when the men began hurling stones at your body?

I'm told that when a person was executed by stoning, there was a pattern the people tended to follow in the execution. Because they wanted the experience to be as painful as possible, they would typically begin by hurling stones at the extremities and body while avoiding the head. This would cause the person to suffer longer before rendering them unconscious. I suspect that this is the kind of treatment Stephen received from this angry crowd. But look at what he did while they were destroying his body and intentionally inflicting as much pain on him as they could:

> As they were stoning Stephen, he called out,
> "Lord Jesus, receive my spirit." And falling to
> his knees he cried out with a loud voice,
> "Lord, do not hold this sin against them."
> And when he had said this, he fell asleep.
> (verses 59–60)

While they were still hurting him, Stephen prayed for them. Before breathing his final breath, he asked the Lord not to hold this sin against them. These words and this action on Stephen's part convince me he was a man whose heart was aligned with Christ's.

We all experience pain in our lives. Much of the pain we endure is caused by other people. Pain that is unintentionally inflicted is usually easier to forgive than pain that's inflicted intentionally. But Christ calls us to handle our pain with His strength. He gives us the power we need to pray for those who intentionally hurt us. Doing so is a blessing to them but also aids us in the process of healing.

Stop dwelling on the ways you've been offended.

Remember Christ.

Remember Stephen.

Tell yourself to pray for those who have intentionally hurt you, even those who are still in the midst of causing you pain.

DWELL ON THIS

I will not harbor bitterness, resentment, or outdated offenses. Today I will pray for those who have intentionally hurt me and I will remember the example Christ set for me.

Don't let your heart be troubled.

The Helper, the Holy Spirit, whom
the Father will send in my name,
he will teach you all things and
bring to your remembrance all that
I have said to you. Peace I leave
with you; my peace I give to you.
Not as the world gives do I give to
you. Let not your hearts be
troubled, neither let them be afraid.

—John 14:26–27

Have you ever had such a bad day you wished you were dead?

I have had several days like that, but the first time I truly felt
that way was in seventh grade. That was a weird season of life
for me in many respects, and my grades started reflecting that
fact.

Up to that point, I was a straight A student. I almost never
scored any lower. I still remember one period several years
earlier when my parents were told I had the highest grades in
the school's entire fourth grade. That set a high bar for their

expectations of me, but in seventh grade I popped that bubble, big time.

Our school calendar was divided into quarters. For the first marking period, my grades were great. Same for the second. But things changed during the third quarter. Not coincidentally, that was a particularly difficult stretch of time at home. My parents' marriage had ended several years earlier, and my mother thought it would be a good idea for me to spend more time working at the garage where her boyfriend worked. I was sent to work there nearly every day after school. Most nights, I didn't get home until after eleven.

At the garage, I was taught how to sand, mask, and prep cars for painting. I was also regularly asked to clean vehicle interiors. But while I was learning those tasks, I was surrounded by a host of bad influences that exposed me to a side of life I wasn't fully acquainted with before. I picked up the habit of smoking. I read the filthy magazines the men left around. My language became coarse and vulgar. I stopped treating my younger siblings with respect, and I stopped treating adults with respect. I basically gave up on caring about the things that used to matter to me. I wanted to impress the guys at the garage, and I didn't spend much time thinking about my life outside that building. At the same time, I resented the fact that I was rarely home. I missed the days of coming home from school, doing my homework, eating dinner, watching TV, and going to bed at a normal time.

During the second half of my seventh-grade year, my worst class was Civics—not because I didn't enjoy the subject, but because I felt the need to give the teacher a hard time and didn't turn in my homework. That's hard to admit now, as I love studying history. In fact, after high school I earned a bachelor's degree in education with the goal of becoming a history teacher. Before becoming a pastor, that's what I believed my career was going to be. But you never would have guessed that back then.

When it came time for the third quarter report cards to be released, I was shocked to see something I had never seen before. My teacher gave me a failing grade. That was a new low for me. Up to that point, I'd never failed a class. I'd never even come remotely close to having that happen before, but I knew I had to hand my mother a report card with a "68/F" in Civics. I knew it wasn't going to go well.

My mother was aware that report cards were being released that day, and I dreaded what was going to happen to me when I opened our apartment door. Sure enough, when I opened the door and she saw that grade, she flipped out. Instinctively, I ran back outside because I knew I was in big trouble. Making matters worse, the edge of my brand-new bright-blue winter jacket caught on the doorknob and severely ripped while I was trying to run away. I was in trouble for failing a class, and I knew I'd be in trouble for tearing my coat.

Later that night after returning home, and after being chastised and grounded, I lay down on my bed, very upset. I truly wished I were dead. I couldn't see beyond that moment. It was the worst day of my life. In many ways, I felt as if my life were over. I even remember praying that Jesus would return and take me to be with Him so I could escape the consequences of what I had done.

Now when I look back at that day or retell that story, it almost seems comical to me. It was certainly a very bad day, but from the perspective of time, it feels completely inconsequential and irrelevant. I see it differently now than I did in the moment. When I look back at it, I see a confused kid who was trying to navigate a broken family, bad influences, and his own immaturity. I feel a sense of compassion for younger me when I remember how challenging that season of life really was.

Thankfully, those troubles were for only a season. It all passed. Everything resolved. My life today looks nothing like it looked back then. That season feels like little more than a blip in my life story, but I'm grateful for the ways in which the Lord uses experiences like that to teach us to show compassion for others when they're going through their low moments.

When we're in the midst of trouble, it's hard to think beyond the moment. It's difficult to see past it. Sometimes we mistakenly allow ourselves to believe that our troubles will never go away and that our lives will never improve.

I had a friend in that same Civics class who was also dealing with some difficulties in his life outside school. I don't know all the details of what was going on, but I'm sure it wasn't pleasant. He could identify with my personal challenges, and I certainly identified with his. Sadly, while we were still students at that school, he chose to end his life. At his viewing, I walked up to his open casket and looked at his face. My heart felt heavy for him and for those who loved him. I distinctly remember asking myself, *Why did he think things would never get better?* I think when we're troubled, we become convinced that things will never change.

Do you understand that your troubles are short lived, or are you convinced that things will never get better?

Do you believe that the sense of pain and loss you may be experiencing right now is permanent, or do you have hope that healing and comfort is possible?

In John 14:27, Jesus said, "Let not your hearts be troubled, neither let them be afraid." Why do you suppose He said that? What truth was He attempting to convey to His followers?

John 14 records a conversation Jesus had with His disciples prior to His arrest and crucifixion. The time was approaching when He would be abruptly taken from them. It would seem like the worst day of their lives. They had placed their trust in Jesus, they were convinced He was going to establish His earthly kingdom in the midst of their generation, and they were certain they were about to reign with Him. But Jesus made it clear to them that their expectations weren't fully lining up with the Father's timetable, and He wanted them to be able to come back to these words of comfort (verse 27) after His arrest and murder. He knew they would need this assurance.

Jesus knows we need His assurance as well. He tells us not to let our hearts be troubled. He also tells us we don't need to be afraid. Why does He say that? On what basis can we trade our troubles for trust in Him?

In that same conversation, Jesus assured us that the Holy Spirit would be sent to us. The Spirit would help us. He would teach us. He would enable us to remember the words Jesus spoke during His time on earth. And through faith in Jesus, we would be blessed with genuine peace unlike anything this world can supply. This world offers you trouble, but Jesus offers you security, stability, and rest.

At present, what are you allowing to trouble your heart? Does your sense of security feel threatened by something? Do you feel as though you're lacking the stability you crave? Are you being robbed of your sense of peace and rest?

During our earthly lives, there will regularly be things that come our way that bring trouble with them. In the moment, it may even feel like you're experiencing your worst day. If it's bad enough, you may start to tell yourself that you'd be better off dead. It's not uncommon for our despair to root that deep when we're looking to the world to offer the solutions for what troubles our souls.

Recently, I watched a documentary that chronicled the causes of America's Great Depression in the late 1920s and early 1930s. It was a tragic account that demonstrated the despair many people felt after the crash of the stock market. Some gave up all hope of living when they contemplated the effects this change was going to have on their personal finances. Some ended their lives. Others sank into deep depression. Still others spent the rest of their lives with a sense of financial paranoia. Their greatest hope had been in the value of their investments. They were trying to utilize a worldly tool to satisfy the deepest longings of their souls. It didn't work. It won't work for you, either.

Your security is found in Jesus.

Your stability is found in Jesus.

Your rest is found in Jesus.

Several years ago, I was having a conversation with my friend Ed. He is about twenty-five years older than I, and he was sharing a few things the Lord had taught him throughout the years that have been helpful during his most difficult seasons. He said to me, "One of the things the Lord has helped me realize in my lowest moments is that today's trouble won't last forever. This too shall pass." I think Ed is right.

If your heart is presently troubled and you're feeling as if there's no hope beyond today, please remember the message Jesus has been trying to convey to His disciples for centuries: You don't need to be troubled. You don't need to be afraid. He is present with you to give you the gift of His peace. Receive that gift, and trade your troubles for trust.

This too shall pass.

DWELL ON THIS

I will remind myself that my lowest moments won't last forever. Even in the midst of them, I won't let my heart be troubled because my trust is in Jesus.

The dominant voice your heart hears should not be one of condemnation.

We are of the truth and reassure
our heart before him; for whenever
our heart condemns us, God is
greater than our heart, and he
knows everything.

—1 John 3:19–20

What's the largest group of people you've embarrassed yourself in front of? Twenty? Fifty? One hundred? What if I told you I had a day when I embarrassed myself in front of thousands of people. Literally thousands, all at the same time.

When I was a child, I had all sorts of vocational dreams. One of those was to be on the radio. I liked the idea of being a singer, but I was also fascinated by the thought of being a radio deejay. I pictured myself making a living by playing music, hosting interviews, and telling funny stories between songs.

When I was about six or seven, my parents bought me a tape recorder that I used daily. When I was about ten, I upgraded my equipment and began recording a fake radio show to entertain my sisters. My stage name was Ace, and I would make recordings of my favorite songs mixed with commentary. (A few years ago, we uncovered one of those tapes and I played it for my wife. She hasn't stopped laughing.)

In ninth grade, I took a tour of one of the most popular radio stations in our area. The deejays invited us to be in the studio with them while they were live on the air, and they showed us their system for switching between songs, using the microphones, and interspersing the commercial breaks. I was fascinated by what I saw, and the experience further fed my dream of being on the radio.

When it was time for college, I strongly considered getting a communications or broadcasting degree, but I went in a different direction instead. The dream, however, remained stuck in my head, and after college, while I was working in my church office one afternoon with the radio on, I heard an announcement that I felt was aimed directly at me. I was listening to WRGN, my favorite Christian station in the region, and I heard this: "WRGN is currently searching for a new announcer and production director for the morning hours. If you're interested in applying, please call us to schedule an in-person interview."

I felt a jolt of electricity blast through my body. I was already serving as a full-time pastor, but the church I served paid a very low salary, and this might be an opportunity for me to supplement my income by doing something I'd always dreamed of. I called the station, scheduled an interview, and eagerly anticipated what came next.

The interview with the station manager seemed to go well. Our theological beliefs were in agreement, and I informed him that the church was willing to allow me to have a morning schedule that was flexible enough for me to be at the station by seven thirty when the broadcast day started. The manager took me into the production room and had me record several sample recordings and then said he would get back to me soon with their decision. Within a few days, I received word that I was hired. I was actually going to be a radio announcer!

Before the reins would be fully turned over to me, my predecessor, Dan, was going to spend a couple of weeks mentoring and training me. He taught me how to edit the shows and other spots. He showed me how the computer automation and satellite feeds worked. He gave me a crash course in how to operate the on-air soundboard, and he did his best to help me develop a feel for what it was like to work the computer, soundboard, and on-air mic at the same time while making live announcements. Doing all of that was complicated, and I knew that it was going to take practice to get it right.

Then the day came for me to go live on the air. With Dan standing behind me, I waited for the music to stop and pressed the button to turn my microphone on. Thousands and thousands of people were listening all over northeastern and central Pennsylvania. In that instant, I started to speak, jumbled my words, froze midsentence, and wasn't sure how to recover. Thankfully, Dan came to my rescue. He grabbed the microphone, finished the announcements for me, and timed it perfectly to end right when we were up against a hard break.

Admittedly, I felt foolish. I knew there were people who were rooting for me who were most likely listening. I also didn't think that was a good way for a new announcer to introduce himself to thousands of faithful listeners. It was a big moment for me, but instead of feeling excited, I felt like a bumbling dolt.

Ever have a moment like that? A moment that you were

looking forward to that ultimately ended in embarrassment? When we have those kinds of experiences, we can crush our spirit with self-condemnation or we can take a different approach.

I easily could have condemned myself. I could have preached a graceless message of judgment to my heart. Thankfully, I didn't. There have been plenty of moments when I have harshly criticized myself for my mistakes, but I'm grateful this wasn't one of them. With practice, I gradually became proficient in my responsibilities at the station and truly learned to enjoy that job. But if the dominant voice my heart heard was a voice of condemnation, I don't think I would have lasted much beyond the day I made my first on-air mistakes.

As I've had additional embarrassing situations over the years, I have gradually become more and more appreciative of these words of the apostle John: "We are of the truth and reassure our heart before him; for whenever our heart condemns us, God is greater than our heart, and he knows everything" (1 John 3:19–20). Let's take a moment to dwell on what we're being told in this passage.

John had a reputation for being a very loving church leader. It wouldn't surprise me to learn that over the course of his ministry, many people came to him for counsel and advice. I'm sure a lot of those conversations also involved the confession of outright sin and negligent mistakes. As the Holy Spirit was guiding him, John gave those people godly counsel on how to address the shortcomings they were willing to own up to. He would not have wanted their hearts to be perpetually crushed; rather, he reassured them of the grace and compassion of God toward His repentant children.

In 1 John 3, he stressed the sacrificial love of Christ. He also spoke about the opportunity we're given to demonstrate

Christ's love toward one another. Then he explained how the love of Christ influences our internal dialogue. He tells us that if we are of the truth (which we are through our relationship with Christ), we can have hearts that are reassured before the Lord. We're reassured that we are lovingly accepted by Him in spite of our many mistakes.

But still, our hearts are sometimes better at expressing condemnation than gracious acceptance. Our hearts like to trick us. They have the capacity to deceive us. Instead of dwelling on the joy we have in Christ, we can start repeating the lie that our errors and mistakes are sufficient to remove us from our place in the family of God. I have experienced this form of internal deception many times. I suspect you have as well.

Thankfully, as John stresses, God is greater than our deceitful hearts. When our hearts lie to us, God's truth steps in to expose the falsehood. God knows everything. He knows our errors, acts of rebellion, and mistakes. He also knows that Jesus Christ atoned for our sin on the cross. Jesus bore our sin when He died in our place. Jesus endured the wrath of God for us so we didn't need to live under it any longer. Jesus took our condemnation so we didn't need to remain condemned.

Through faith in Christ, we become the recipients of these blessings.

We become children of God.

We become objects of mercy.

If God no longer says we're condemned, what sense does it make for us to reinforce a message of condemnation to our already redeemed hearts? It isn't logical, it isn't correct, and it isn't helpful. That's why the Holy Spirit inspired John to remind us that God is greater than our self-condemnation. If God says we're no longer condemned once we've trusted in

Christ, it would be contradictory to the truth of His Word for us to tell ourselves otherwise.

The dominant voice your heart needs to hear is the voice of grace and truth. The more acquainted you become with the teaching of Scripture and the more adept you become at heeding the voice of the Holy Spirit when He speaks to you, the more likely you'll begin to speak to your heart the way He speaks. The lies of self-condemnation won't hold the same power over your perspective when your heart becomes filled with the truth the Spirit reveals.

It's entirely possible that your biggest mistakes are behind you. It's also possible that your past mistakes were just the opening act to the grandest mistake you've yet to make. Maybe you'll even have an audience of thousands to hear or observe you when you make your error. If and when that day comes, what are you going to tell yourself in the aftermath of that blunder? Will the words you preach to your heart align with the truth God has revealed?

DWELL ON THIS

> The dominant voice my heart hears doesn't need to be a voice of condemnation. Through Jesus, I have been rescued and redeemed. He has paid too costly a price on my behalf for me to tell myself anything less. Today I will listen to a voice of grace.

There is greater joy in giving than in consuming.

In all things I have shown you that
by working hard in this way we
must help the weak and remember
the words of the Lord Jesus, how
he himself said, "It is more blessed
to give than to receive."

—*Acts 20:35*

More and more, the Lord has been teaching me to listen to His voice and obey His prompting, even when what He's prompting me to do doesn't seem to make much sense and even if obedience will cost me something. Early in the process of planting our church, I started to sense that He was nudging me in a particular direction that would force me to be generous with my time, and He convinced me that He wanted me to act on His leading.

The nudge He was giving me was to start a youth ministry at our newly planted church. At that point, our congregation consisted of a small group of people. Several had young children, but none of the families had teens. The timing seemed strange, but I figured that if this was what He wanted, He would send teens in our direction. And that's exactly what He did within two weeks of first impressing the idea in my mind.

I was standing in our parking lot one evening around dinnertime when three teens came running through. Several years later, they admitted to me they were running from the police, who were chasing them because of vandalism on the building next to our church. I was completely unaware of that in the moment, and I asked the kids if I could chat with them. I asked them, "If I carve out time to start a youth group for teens at this church that meets on Sunday nights at six, do you think you and your friends might attend?" They said yes. (I later learned they were using me for cover from the police.) I gave them some of my business cards and asked them to give those cards to their parents so I could talk to them too. The following week when the youth group started, nine teens, including the original three, showed up. I could see God's hand in it all, and I was grateful to watch it grow.

As the teens got to know me and the other adult volunteers, they started nagging me to take the group on a trip to an amusement park. They were persistent. They'd talk about it every week, stop by the church at random times to make their requests, and had even started a small social-media campaign to persuade me to say yes. Of course, I always intended to take them, but because I was getting a kick out of their persistence, I let the suspense drag on for a while. When I finally agreed, they were thrilled.

Most amusement parks in our region are ridiculously expensive. I guess the costs of running a large park with many complicated rides and high insurance rates make that inevitable. I knew that our trip wasn't going to be cheap, but about a month before it was to happen, I received a promotional coupon in the mail that would give us a major discount on ticket prices. In fact, the park sent me two coupons. I knew we'd be able to use only one, but I brought the extra coupon with me anyway. Our group was large, so the amount we saved was significant, which was a huge blessing, and I hoped to share the second coupon as a blessing for someone else.

At the park, after we paid to enter, I hung around the payment booths for a few extra minutes. I prayed, *Lord, please show me who I'm supposed to give this extra coupon to.* Then I spotted them. Several booths to the left of ours, I saw a mother, a grandmother, and two children who were in the process of paying to enter the park. I ran up to them while they were talking to the cashier and said, "Wait! Did you pay yet?" The mother replied, "Yes, I just swiped my card." Then I handed her the coupon and said, "See if they'll still let you use this." The cashier agreed, scanned the coupon, and reduced the woman's fee by $110. She was stunned and quite grateful.

As she walked away, I heard the older woman she was with ask her, "What did that man want?" She said, "He just gave me something that saved us over a hundred dollars!" They both looked surprised and grateful, and they just stood in place looking at each other. I'm glad the Lord allowed me to overhear that part of their conversation.

For the rest of that day, I rode all kinds of impressive rides and had a lot of fun with our group. But now, more than a decade later, the primary memory I have of that day was the joy I experienced through sharing a small blessing with another family. It was small in the sense that it didn't really cost me anything, but not small in the impression it left on my heart. A major theme park catered to my desire for entertainment all day, yet the greatest joy I experienced was triggered by something the Lord allowed me to share with someone else. It truly is more blessed to give than to receive.

That's precisely what Jesus modeled and taught during His earthly ministry. There isn't a single thing we can offer Him that is better than what He has given us. He left the glories of heaven to walk upon this sin-cursed earth. He left His place of honor to be dishonored and unappreciated by men. He left comfort behind so He could suffer and die in our place. But He did this all with a view toward the future. He knew He would rise from death and share His victory over the grave with all who trusted in Him. He knew that in temporarily leaving His place of honor and comfort, He could make us partakers of His glory and offer us the comforts of eternity in His presence.

In Acts 20, when Paul was speaking to the elders of the Ephesian church, he made a point to remind them of the words of Christ: "In all things I have shown you that by working hard in this way we must help the weak and remember the words of the Lord Jesus, how he himself said, 'It is more blessed to give than to receive'" (verse 35). Paul was working to weave Christ's attitude into his own. He was encouraging the leaders in Ephesus to do the same. And as we read these words, we're also invited to welcome the teaching of Christ into our lives. His teaching is so different from what we typically experience in this world. His way of thinking isn't the kind that dominates our consumption-obsessed culture.

Overconsumption is an issue that we might wrestle with, particularly if we live in an affluent society. Many people use consumption as a means to fill a spiritual void in their lives. A while back, a friend of mine commented online, "I tried to eat one cookie from this box, but somehow I ate the entire thing." I laughed when I read that because it sounded strangely familiar. If one cookie makes me happy, maybe an entire box will make me extra happy!

How many people do you know who needlessly update their wardrobe several times a year? Why do they do it? Are they convinced they'll finally discover what's missing from their lives through their attire?

I know a man who spent most of his adult life buying a new car every year. I use the term *buying* loosely, as he never actually paid them off. He just kept rolling the balance of the previous vehicle into the new one. As long as he kept making the payments, the dealers enabled his needless upgrades. On his days off, he would wander around car lots, looking at new vehicles. Finally, I asked him, "Do you suppose you're doing this as a way to help you cope with unwanted pain in other areas of your life?" To my surprise, he answered me honestly and said, "Yes. I think that's true."

Food, clothing, and cars are all nice, but their value deteriorates quickly. Right now, a friend who owns a car dealership is selling a BMW that originally retailed for $121,000 six years ago. It has only 27,000 miles on it, and he's selling it for $40,000. Whoever bought it when it was new effectively spent more than $80,000 to drive it less than 5,000 miles a year, then got rid of it when it stopped satisfying his or her emotional need.

Scripture reveals to us that there is greater joy in giving than in consuming. As Christ has generously blessed us, He calls us to generously bless others. He invites and empowers us to adopt His mindset as our own. Receiving is wonderful, but giving is an even greater blessing:

> As for the rich in this present age, charge
> them not to be haughty, nor to set their
> hopes on the uncertainty of riches, but on

God, who richly provides us with everything
to enjoy. They are to do good, to be rich in
good works, to be generous and ready to
share, thus storing up treasure for themselves as a good foundation for the future, so
that they may take hold of that which is truly
life. (1 Timothy 6:17–19)

One gives freely, yet grows all the richer;
    another withholds what he should give,
      and only suffers want.
Whoever brings blessing will be enriched,
    and one who waters will himself be watered.
(Proverbs 11:24–25)

The Lord will meet our needs. I believe there are many
things He allows us to be temporary stewards of for the express purpose of sharing the blessing with others. We don't
give with the goal of receiving something in return; we give
as people who have been blessed in more ways than we can
count. Giving is good for the soul. Through it, the Lord allows
us to experience a part of His heart that we might not notice
or appreciate otherwise.

Life isn't about what you covet or consume. If you're convinced you'll find contentment through consumption or ac-
quisition, you'll be deeply disappointed. Jesus said there's a
greater blessing in giving than in receiving. He will help you
understand the difference between the two if you let Him.

Let your soul be content with Christ.

Hold loosely to the transient things of this world.

Give as the Lord compels you to do so.

DWELL ON THIS

Greater joy comes in giving than in receiving, so today
I will look for opportunities to bless others just as I
have been blessed.

The Lord delights in you when you work and when you rest.

There remains a Sabbath rest for
the people of God, for whoever has
entered God's rest has also rested
from his works as God did from
his.

—*Hebrews 4:9–10*

Growing up in an entrepreneurial family was a gift. I was surrounded by people who valued working hard, taking risks, and keeping yourself motivated. From a very early age, I discovered that I enjoyed spending time in my father's grocery store, and I wanted to work there as much as he would let me.

I'm grateful that labor laws apparently don't apply to family businesses. (At least I don't think they do.) And if they did back in the 1980s, no one told my father. He let me do all kinds of jobs in his store from a very young age, and he paved a path for me to develop a work ethic that continues to serve me well.

One of the major tasks in a grocery store is "conditioning," or "facing," the shelves. Someone has to do it, and it's usually the stock boy. When I was ten years old, my father taught me what conditioning was and how to do it well. He put a duster in my hand and said, "I want you to go through this entire aisle, bring all the stock to the front of the shelf, remove any dust, and position the labels so they're facing out. You have one hour to complete this aisle, and if I find more than ten items not perfectly arranged, I'm docking you one hour's pay."

To be honest, I thought this task was going to be easy, until I actually gave it a try. First of all, dust is invisible to a ten-year-old boy, so I'm glad he wasn't grading me on how much I failed to brush away. Then I realized I needed better balancing skills to do this job well. Some of the items needed to be stacked on top of each other, but back then, certain brands of canned goods and other items weren't designed to do that. (Now they taper the bottoms of cans so they fit inside the lid of the can underneath them.) Making it even more complicated was that people were shopping, and as soon as I would get a section finished, someone would inevitably buy a few things and upset my displays.

At the end of the hour, my father came around the corner and asked, "Well, are you ready?" I thought I was, until he started walking down the aisle and pointing out items I had missed or didn't bring right up to the edge. He started counting, "One, two, three . . ."

This wasn't good. He was barely through the first section of the aisle and had already found three items not perfectly conditioned. His count continued: "Four, five, six . . ." I was getting nervous. I had spent so much time trying to make the aisle perfect, but his trained eye was catching all sorts of things I hadn't seen. I also knew he didn't make empty threats. If he found ten misplaced items, he really would dock my pay.

He continued his stroll through the aisle and stopped in front of the final section. "Seven, eight, nine . . ." At that point, I had given up hope. For sure he was going to find something else I'd missed. I had worked hard at conditioning the shelves, but it was my first time attempting the task and I was starting to feel as though I had just wasted an entire hour. But his count never reached ten. He looked at the aisle and said, "This was a good first try. You missed less than ten items, so I'm pleased. Now that you know how to do this properly, start conditioning the rest of the aisles as well."

It felt good to have my father's approval. I think every son craves it deep down. And somewhere inside me, I started to associate fatherly approval with hard work. If you work hard, your father will be pleased. If you slack off, he won't be. It seemed like a simple equation to me.

Our relationships with our fathers tend to affect our perceptions of our heavenly Father, whether we want to admit that or not. If you've had a healthy relationship with your father, you'll probably give God the benefit of the doubt and think of Him in loving terms. If you've had an unpleasant relationship with your father, you'll probably have to spend some time examining how that relationship has influenced your view of God in order to make sure you aren't making incorrect assumptions about His nature.

Earthly fathers need to be aware of the ways they affect their children's perception of God. As a father, I wrestle with this reality frequently because I know I'm a work in progress. I get some things right, but I also get many things wrong. I try to share the wisdom I have with my children, but that knowledge base is always developing and maturing. The version of me that exists ten years from now will be much wiser than the version of me that's raising them at present. I frequently pray for wisdom and the Lord's help to do the job well. Thankfully, love covers a multitude of mistakes.

To their credit, my children are all hard workers. The work ethic that was drilled into me has been drilled into them. And as I tend to hold down multiple jobs at once, I see them doing the same. I frequently praise them for this, but there's one glaring deficiency in my parenting that I haven't excelled at modeling for them: I have done a much better job at teaching them the value of work than I have at teaching them the value of rest.

One of the most common false gospels we're tempted to preach is that of works-based righteousness. I am in the midst of a lifelong journey of overcoming this false belief. We mistakenly believe that God delights in His children only when they're working or doing something of noticeable consequence. But Scripture teaches us that God values rest as well. He encourages us to find ultimate rest through faith in Christ, and He delights in us whether we're working or resting.

The writer of Hebrews said, "There remains a Sabbath rest for the people of God, for whoever has entered God's rest has also rested from his works as God did from his" (4:9–10). The first time I examined that passage closely was during my junior year of college. I remember admitting to myself, *I don't know what this means.*

What is a Sabbath rest?

How does someone enter God's rest?

Does God really want me to rest from work?

The context of that passage describes the children of Israel's experience of entering into the Promised Land after decades of wandering in the wilderness. They wandered for forty years because they struggled to trust God's teaching, leading, and love. The first generation of adults who left Egypt

during the exodus were told they would not enter the Promised Land because of their hard-hearted unbelief. It would be
their children who would experience rest from their wandering in a beautiful land the Lord had prepared for them.

That historical example was used to illustrate a deeper
spiritual reality that we should take hold of today. Many people wander through life struggling to trust the Lord. They
question His goodness. They question His motives. They're
skeptical of the idea that He providentially works all things
together for the good of His children. They may even doubt
that He desires to be a Father to them. And if they do believe
He exists, they're convinced they need to work to earn His
loving approval.

When asked if they think He will accept them into His
eternal presence, they say things like "I sure hope so." When
asked why, they run through the list of what they've done.
They've worked. They've toiled. They've stacked. They've
dusted. They've conditioned because they know the day is
coming when God is going to start counting.

If that sounds similar to our perspective toward God, that
also means we trust more in the work of our hands than in
His hand to save us.

The kind of Sabbath rest the writer of Hebrews was trying
to teach us about is the kind of rest people experience only
when they realize they don't have to spend decades wandering through life trying to earn God's approval. We will never
be at peace or at rest until we accept that all the work that
needed to be done in order for us to be approved by God was
done by Jesus. He lived the perfect life for us, atoned for our
sin, and rose from the grave because we were incapable of
doing these things. Now He asks us to trust in Him and receive the assurance of knowing that His approval is our ap-

proval. As God the Father sees God the Son, so too does He see all those who are in Christ.

This means that God delights in you when you're resting and when you're working.

How many decades have you spent telling yourself that God doesn't delight in you? How have you allowed the ways in which fallible humans show each other approval to distort your understanding of God's approval?

You're allowed to take a break. If you've been working non-stop because you're convinced that your value is tied to the work you do, it would be quite healthy for you to balance your work with rest.

Your efforts are not what give you value in God's eyes. He loves you when you glorify Him through the work of your hands, and He loves you when you take time to appreciate the work He has done on your behalf through His Son.

When you work, do so as someone who knows he or she is already approved. When you rest, do so as one who is grateful for the peace that floods a heart that learns to trust.

You can't stack the cans perfectly. Don't spend the rest of your life convinced that your value in God's kingdom is tied to the work of your hands.

DWELL ON THIS

Work is a privilege, and rest is a gift. Today I will work and rest because I know the Lord delights in me doing both.

Trade your fears for confidence in God.

All who are led by the Spirit of God
are sons of God. For you did not
receive the spirit of slavery to fall
back into fear, but you have
received the Spirit of adoption as
sons, by whom we cry, "Abba!
Father!"

—*Romans* 8:14–15

When someone says, "Hey, would you be willing to do a favor for me?" get the details before you blindly agree. In college I was asked to do one of those favors and quickly came to regret it.

A few months before the end of my first year of college, I met Andrea. I was certain she was going to be my wife someday, and that's exactly what she became. We didn't think that it made sense for us to get married while we were finishing our degrees, so we intended to get married as soon as we were done. There was just one problem with that plan: she is a year older than I am and would be finished a full year ahead of my academic schedule. So I devised a plan that would allow me to finish college a semester early. I received permission from the school administration to take twenty-one credits during the semesters and an extra nine credits during the summer for two successive summers. That plan worked, and the day after my final class, we got married.

But getting to that point was a little bumpy. Summer semesters on campus were strange. The place was like a ghost town, with just a few random people remaining in the dorms. I roomed with my friend Al, who was taking some of the same classes I was.

Al was an interesting guy who had a gift for making me laugh. He liked to snack on animal crackers. But he had a curious habit that I noticed when he was eating them. He would bite off the animal's head, then throw the bottom half away. When I asked him why, he said with a straight face, "I don't eat the butts."

Al is a New Jersey state trooper now, so he's the epitome of a law-abiding citizen, but during our college years, he liked to stretch the rules a little. As student supervision was rather minimal during the summer, Al decided to sneak a pet into our dorm. One afternoon I came back from class and found a large aquarium against the wall in our room. I asked him, "What's that for?" He told me, "I have a friend who is giving me a python." Later that day, the python arrived and moved into the room with us.

Al loved that snake. I was a little concerned that she might sneak out of the aquarium and kill us. He didn't seem very worried. He brought her outside our dorm one afternoon and asked a young girl who was on campus to suggest a name for her. She suggested Sugar Cookie. So that's what we called the python from that point on. I also knew which end of the snake Al was most likely to eat in a survival situation and which end he was likely to leave for me.

Partway through the summer semester, Al had to go out of town for most of a week. That's when he asked me for a small favor. "Hey, Stange! While I'm gone, would you be willing to feed Sugar Cookie? I'll leave some money for you to pick up a mouse at the pet store. And if you don't mind, take her out of the aquarium a few times and rub her back. I want her to stay used to human interaction."

Like a dummy, I said, "Um, okay."

So, in keeping with my agreement, I went to the pet store the next day and bought a mouse. Al advised me to use a set of tongs when I lowered the mouse into the aquarium so Sugar Cookie wouldn't unintentionally bite my hand. I have to admit that I felt really bad for that mouse as it went sniffing around that aquarium. Once or twice, it came up to the snake's head. Sugar Cookie was alerted to the mouse's presence, and before I knew it, she struck, constricted, then forced the mouse down her neck. Part one of the favor was now complete.

The next day, I decided to take Sugar Cookie out of the aquarium. I placed her across the back of my neck and let the rest of her body drape down my left arm. While she rested there, I slowly stroked her scales. Sugar Cookie sometimes had trouble shedding, and there was a small patch on her back that didn't shed properly. She didn't like that part being touched, but unfortunately, I stopped paying close attention to what I was doing after a few minutes and accidentally bumped that spot.

In that moment, Sugar Cookie quickly lifted her head up and whipped her neck in my direction so she could stare at me eye to eye. It was very abrupt, which gave me the impression she was angry. Then she just stared at me as though she were going to give me the same treatment she gave the mouse one day earlier. Her face was about four inches from mine, and I completely froze. I didn't want to do anything that might cause her to snap at me or constrict herself around my neck. I didn't blink. I took quiet and deliberate breaths and waited for her to calm down. I was frozen with fear.

Thankfully, after an intense stare-off, she started to relax again and gradually lowered her head. When her head dipped low enough, I lifted her off my neck, put her back in the aquarium, latched the lid, and said out loud, "Next time, take care of your own stupid snake!"

Fear isn't a pleasant emotional response, and it can be a debilitating force in our lives. If not for our confidence in God's sovereign power, we might be highly tempted to live in fear. I think my fear of that python was a natural one that most people would agree was logical, but there have been many other forms of fear that I have allowed to creep into my life that were far from healthy.

In Romans 8:15, Paul taught us that if we're being led by the Spirit of God, we can be confident that we have been received into the family of God as His children. We are loved. We are valued. We have a position of esteem in the sense that He has given us His name and an incorruptible inheritance in His kingdom. We aren't hired hands in His household. We aren't slaves who have been brought into His presence against our will. We have been adopted into God's family and can approach Him with the affection of children who are convinced they're deeply loved.

That's the way God sees us, and our relationship with Him is secured the moment we come to faith in Jesus, so we don't need to fall back into the fear of being rejected by Him. We don't need to be immobilized by the thought that God is going to change His mind about us, rescind His grace, return us to a state of condemnation, or remove us from His family.

Living in fear of God's judgment makes sense if we haven't experienced the pardon for sin that comes through faith in Christ. But Paul reminds us that if we have received that pardon, we don't need to fall back into fear. The fear of condemnation is the fear of a slave, not the faith of a son. It's a fear that forgets the steep price the Lord paid to adopt us into His family. There are many problems with fear:

Falling back into fear feeds your insecurity. Insecure people are always seeking validation, often in unhealthy ways. This kind of insecurity reminds me of people who post selfies online in the hopes that someone, anyone, will tell them they're attractive.

Falling back into fear robs you of the joy of a new perspective. Now that you've been adopted into the family of God, you're viewed differently by Him. You were once on the outside; now you're on the inside. Why live like an outsider? Why embrace the perspective of someone who isn't sure he or she belongs? What value is there in preaching that falsehood to your heart?

Falling back into fear keeps you living in a past that's no longer relevant to you. It's true that you were once an object of God's wrath, but when you came to know Christ, that changed. Through Jesus, you're a recipient of mercy, with a glorious future ahead of you. Do you really want to spend the rest of your years paralyzed by the kind of fearful mentality that would be more fitting for someone who doesn't know where he or she is headed? Your life has purpose now. Your life has direction. You don't need to remain caught in an irrelevant past.

A few months after Andrea and I got married, there was a small fire in our kitchen. Andrea was frying vegetables, and the oil ignited. Instinctively, she grabbed the pan and placed it in the sink, but the flames continued to rise and caught the curtains above our sink on fire. She screamed and froze.

I was in the next room and could hear the sound of the flames and her scream, so I immediately ran into the kitchen, fearing that she had been burned. Thankfully, she was fine, but the fire was growing. I opened the refrigerator, grabbed a box of baking soda, and spread the powder on the flames to smother them. When everything calmed down and our hearts stopped racing, we were grateful that the only thing we needed to do was purchase new curtains and touch up some damaged paint.

Afterward, Andrea was mad at herself. It bothered her that she froze in fear instead of taking action. Sadly, that's the way many people spend their entire lives. They remain frozen in fear instead of walking by faith. They're petrified because they haven't embraced the security of their positions in God's family. They fail to take action because they can't shake the mindset of slavery.

I can't blame you if a python creeps you out. They creep me out too. I can't blame you if an uncontrolled fire raging through your kitchen causes you to panic. That can happen to the best of us. But don't fall back into the paralysis of spiritual fear after Christ has set you free. To do so means you're failing to understand the nature of the new life you've been granted through Him.

In Christ, you are part of God's family forever. Tell yourself you can approach each day with the confidence and assurance that your position in His family affords.

DWELL ON THIS

Through Christ, my position in the family of God is secure. Today I will look for ways to trade my fears for confidence in God.

Focus on issues that truly matter.

Have nothing to do with foolish, ignorant controversies; you know that they breed quarrels. And the Lord's servant must not be quarrelsome but kind to everyone, able to teach, patiently enduring evil.

—2 Timothy 2:23–24

Over the past few decades, I have officiated for many marriage ceremonies. When people ask me to perform their ceremony, I have a list of requirements they need to agree to. After reading my list, most people choose to ask someone else to be their officiant. I'm totally fine with that because I don't really enjoy most weddings. I'd probably like them more if people kept them simple, but there's a great deal of pressure on couples to meet certain social expectations and show off, and that makes me feel uncomfortable when I have to sit through it.

I am, however, a huge fan of marriage. I think a healthy marriage can provide one of the clearest earthly examples of the love of Christ for His bride, the church. So when I'm asked to be part of a couple's wedding, my primary concern is for the long-term strength of their union. I want their marriage to last. I want them to honor the covenant they inaugurate before God and their family. I want to contribute toward setting them up for success to the best of my ability. So, when they ask me to officiate, one of the things my list requires is multiple sessions of counseling in the months prior to the ceremony. Some people really balk at that stipulation.

I once turned down a request to officiate for a woman who called me on a Tuesday asking if I could conduct her wedding that Friday. I said, "I'm sorry, but I can't help you with this. I require the bride and groom to go through months of premarital counseling before I can officiate their wedding."

She replied, "This is my fourth wedding. I know all there is to know about marriage. There isn't anything new you'd be able to teach me." I held my tongue, but you can guess what I really wanted to say.

One of my favorite things to do when a couple sits down with me for their first counseling session is invite them to share the topic of their most recent argument. Almost without exception, they immediately look at each other, give a half smile, tilt their heads down, squint their eyes, and say, "Do we really have to tell you what it was about? It's pretty embarrassing."

Up to this point, I have never had a couple say to me, "Well, as we drove to your office, we had a heated debate about world peace, nuclear demilitarization, sustainable tree harvesting, and the inherent nature of humanity." Inevitably, they say something like, "Our most recent argument was over whether pasta noodles taste different based on their shape. She says they don't. I say they do."

I'm amazed at how fruitless most arguments really are. When people argue, the debate tends to be driven more by their desire to win than by their desire to persuade. They throw verbal jabs and knockout punches as they try to make their points. They deal a few low blows as well by throwing in a few insults. In the end, they celebrate (momentarily) if the other person gives up. They win the argument at the cost of the relationship.

But has God called us to be argumentative? Have you and I been given mouths so we can use them to quarrel with others?

The New Testament books Paul addressed to Timothy and Titus are frequently called the pastoral epistles. In those letters, Paul offers sound counsel to these two men who were serving as pastors during the days of the early church. One of my favorite aspects of studying those letters is the counsel the Holy Spirit inspired Paul to share about being a person of character in the midst of a character-starved generation.

In 2 Timothy 2:23–24, Paul advised Timothy, "Have nothing to do with foolish, ignorant controversies; you know that they breed quarrels. And the Lord's servant must not be quarrelsome but kind to everyone, able to teach, patiently enduring evil." When I read good advice like that, I wonder what it would look like if I truly took it to heart.

Timothy was instructed to have nothing to do with foolish and ignorant controversies. Every few years, there seems to be a new controversy over something inconsequential that grips people's attention. People take sides, cut each other down, and forget that the Lord has called us to edify each other. Winning fruitless debates becomes more important to us than building each other up in truth and love, so we take the bait and tear each other apart in the process.

Timothy was also warned that foolish arguments breed

quarrels. I'm convinced that Satan loves breeding disunity and quarrels among God's people. Instead of combining our efforts, investing our gifts in each other, and focusing on what really matters, we quarrel and divide. And while we waste our time fighting each other, reaching the lost world with the hope of the gospel becomes an afterthought.

What's God's calling on your life? Do you consider yourself His servant? If you're in any form of church leadership, that certainly should be your perspective. But even if you aren't a leader with an official title, I think it's healthy to consider yourself a servant of the Lord wherever He stations you.

According to Scripture, the Lord's servant must not be quarrelsome. I think this counsel speaks to both our attitudes and what we choose to participate in. We shouldn't be looking for inconsequential issues to argue about, and we don't need to attend every quarrel we're invited to.

We're also plainly told that the Lord's servant must be kind to everyone. The kindness we demonstrate will reflect on the Lord we claim to represent. As people who are filled with the Holy Spirit, our temperaments should remain under His control. The Spirit-empowered temperament we demonstrate will be used by the Lord to promote and preserve peace among His family.

I think it's also quite interesting that in the same grouping of verses that tell us that the Lord's servant should have nothing to do with foolish controversies that breed quarreling, we're also told that the Lord's servant must be able to teach. This is something the Lord grants leaders in the church the opportunity and responsibility to do. They instruct others in the teaching of God's Word. They serve as models of how the teaching of the Bible should be put into practice. Sound teaching matters to the Lord, but how can someone teach if he or she isn't first teachable? If we foster a quarrelsome attitude, we'll become poor listeners who reject wisdom when it's offered to us. And if we make a habit of rejecting godly wisdom, we will disqualify ourselves from being entrusted to teach and influence others.

God's Word also reveals that the Lord's servant is to exhibit patience toward others whose eyes have not yet been opened to the truth. If you're a fully devoted follower of Christ, you possess a power that isn't being accessed by those who don't yet believe. You provide a contrast to the perspective of those who embrace their disbelief. Their eyes are still unable to see their need for Jesus. But if you're more concerned with winning arguments than in demonstrating the transformative power of Christ, you'll find yourself beating down the very people Christ has sent you to lift up. There are certain seasons of life that can make this principle rather clear.

I'm at one of those dangerous seasons of life. I'm old enough to know valuable things and still young enough to have the strength to help others. There are people who are leaning on me from multiple directions. The generation below leans on me, as does the generation above. I support my children and assist my parents.

When people depend on you for help, you become convinced that you have permission to offer your opinions. What's the best way to advise your son about politics once he's old enough to vote? How can you convince your father not to buy a certain car when he can clearly remember the pieces of junk you chose to drive in high school?

There are issues worth disagreeing about, but I don't see the value in being disagreeable when doing so.

I think there are situations and opinions we would love to change if we could, but it doesn't help to drive ourselves crazy through arguing. We're called to speak the truth in love, not in a spirit of self-righteous argumentation. We're called to teach and pray while giving room for the Holy Spirit to change us over time. Tell yourself that He can be trusted to do His job.

When we learn to focus on the issues that truly matter, we'll be able to set foolishness aside. We won't feel as compelled to waste our energy on minor matters that have more power to divide than to build up.

So, what is Christ calling us to focus on? I think we're called to focus on the same things He is.

We're called to give the Father glory, not covet glory for ourselves. We're called to remain confident in His unmatchable power and perfect plan.

We're to serve and sacrifice for others as Christ has done for us. We do so in view of the hope He holds secure for all who trust in Him.

We're called to build one another up as the Holy Spirit is presently building us up. We comfort, teach, assist, and encourage with the strength He supplies.

The Lord has sent us into this world as His agents of grace, not as ambassadors of foolishness. Don't waste your words or your time. Remain focused on the calling that Christ has given you as His servant.

DWELL ON THIS

Today I will focus on issues that truly matter because Christ has called me to be an agent of His grace.

Value listening as much as you value speaking.

Let every person be quick to hear,
slow to speak, slow to anger.

—*James* 1:19

One Sunday morning as I was preparing to step onto the platform to preach, I caught something out of the corner of my eye that I didn't expect to see: a man was sitting on a chair in our entryway with his head resting on his hands. As I looked a little closer, I could see that he was crying. I had just a few moments before I needed to begin preaching, but I wanted to check in on him first.

I walked over to him and asked, "Are you okay?" He didn't verbally reply but shook his head no. I continued, "Would you be willing to stick around to chat a little after I'm done speaking?" He shrugged his shoulders. Then I said, "I really hope you'll stick around, but for now, let me pray for you." We prayed together, and then I walked up front to share that morning's message. Afterward, I found the man and invited him to sit down and talk. He agreed, so we found an unused corner of the room and talked for a while.

Actually, I probably shouldn't say we talked. He did most of the talking, and I listened. For about two hours he shared some pressing concerns that were hitting his family hard. The primary issue he was wrestling with was his marriage, but there were other issues weighing his heart down as well.

In one moment, he was sad. In the next, he was angry. Then grief-stricken, determined, confused, and resolute. His emotions were all over the place, but I sat and listened while he unloaded what had been upsetting him. In the following weeks, I met with him and his wife and we attempted to reconcile differences and work through the difficult process of forgiveness and restoration.

As we were talking, I wanted both of them to know they had my undivided attention. I made eye contact, shook my head, and said "hmm" and "uh-huh" while they told their stories. Because many marriages in crisis consist of two parties who don't feel heard, I wanted to make an extra effort to convey my desire to hear exactly what they had to say. The importance of taking that posture was illustrated for me by another pastor several decades earlier—one I met through my wife.

My wife grew up in a very good church. Soon after we started dating, I had the opportunity to visit her church and meet some of the wonderful people she had been telling me about. She introduced me to many people who played roles in her spiritual formation, including her pastors. There were two pastors on staff at the time, and both had excellent people skills. One of them in particular seemed to excel at connecting with people of all ages. I said to Andrea, "He strikes me as a good leader. What stands out to you about him?"

She said, "When you're talking to him, he stays focused on what you're saying. He doesn't abandon the conversation or look away. It's always abundantly clear that he's listening to you and intentionally interacting with what you're communicating. He always makes you feel like he's interested in what you have to say."

I think being a good listener is a real gift, and it's certainly something Scripture teaches us to value. In James 1:19, we're encouraged to be "quick to hear." The book of James places a high emphasis on the value of wisdom and living out our faith in practical ways. So, what's wise about being quick to hear? What was James instructing us about how we're called to live out our faith?

James was teaching us that one of the signs of spiritual maturity among followers of Christ is the conscious decision to communicate to others that they're valued. Christ has made it clear that we are valued by Him and that we should likewise convey that same attitude to others. We can tell each other that we value one another, but those words don't carry as much meaning when they aren't intentionally demonstrated. That means that if I value you, I'll make a point to value what you say. I may not always agree, but I don't need to rush to be the next person to talk the second you take a breath. Sometimes one of the best ways we can convey genuine love is through listening to each other.

One evening during my college years, I got a phone call that I wasn't looking forward to receiving. My great-aunt, someone who had been like a bonus grandmother to me, had been in the hospital attempting to recover from the effects of a stroke. She'd had several strokes in the past, but this one was the worst yet. I had driven several hours to visit with her a few days earlier, and it became clear to me that she might not pull through. When I received the phone call that confirmed she had passed, I wasn't shocked, but I was certainly sad.

When someone I love passes away, I become instantly nostalgic. I start reflecting on all the experiences I had with him or her and the conversations we shared. That evening when I received the news of my great-aunt's death, I walked over to my dorm and told one of my good friends the sad news. I mentioned to him how important she had been in my life and what a blessing she was to my sisters and me. I shared these details while my friend was lying on his bed, but I stopped talking when he started snoring. While I was express-ing my grief, he fell asleep! I couldn't believe he did that. His inability to stay awake and listen amplified the pain I was feel-ing. It was nearly impossible for me to be willing to share anything of a deeper nature with him after that experience.

I'm grateful the Lord listens to the pleas we bring before Him. I'm also grateful He completely understands how it feels to have friends who don't listen and instead fall asleep when we're grieving.

Just before His crucifixion, Jesus took His disciples to the Garden of Gethsemane. Scripture tells us that Jesus was sor-rowful and troubled. He knew what was coming next and wanted to spend time in prayer to the Father in preparation for His betrayal and execution. He instructed the disciples to remain watchful and pray as well, but instead of listening, they fell asleep.

> He came to the disciples and found them sleeping. And he said to Peter, "So, could you not watch with me one hour?" (Matthew 26:40)

Why is listening so hard for us to do? Why are we sur-prised when we meet someone who's actually a good listener? Should that trait be as rare as it is?

Have you ever considered what might be at the root of our struggle to actually listen in a careful, thoughtful, and intentional way?

We like being heard, but we have a difficult time hearing. This demonstrates just how wrapped up in ourselves we can easily become. It's evidence of the presence of self-destructive pride. Our aversion to listening robs us of growth and wisdom.

When the apostle Paul was planting churches and training new believers, he did a lot of teaching. Some of the people he taught were very eager to hear what he had to say; others were not as interested, and they demonstrated that with their occasional defiance or obvious slumber.

> A young man named Eutychus, sitting at the window, sank into a deep sleep as Paul talked still longer. And being overcome by sleep, he fell down from the third story and was taken up dead. (Acts 20:9)

One of the churches that prompted Paul to experience great joy was the church at Philippi. In his letter to them, Paul said, "What you have learned and received and heard and seen in me—practice these things, and the God of peace will be with you" (Philippians 4:9). Before they could be doers of the Word, they first needed to be hearers of it. Paul admonished the church to practice what they'd learned, received, and heard from him. He showed them what it was like to receive godly counsel and put it into practice. He was inviting them to set their pride aside and implement instruction that was being given to them through a reliable source.

What kind of relationship do you think you would have

with the Lord if He never demonstrated a willingness to hear you as you poured out your heart to Him?

What kind of relationship do you think you would have with Him if you never listened to what He said to you?

The willingness to listen demonstrates the depth of trust and respect that's present in a relationship. I communicate love to my wife and children when I listen to them. I communicate disinterest and disrespect when I don't. I communicate love for my church family when I listen to them. I communicate aloofness when I don't.

We all want to be heard, but sometimes it can be far too easy to talk without listening. When we do so, we might miss genuine opportunities to glean wisdom and insight from others. We also lose the chance to make someone else feel valued and appreciated.

In Christ, we are loved, valued, and appreciated. We are heard, and His willingness to hear us reassures us that a divinely ordained relationship has been established between us. We confess to Him and communicate with Him because we know He listens.

If you're someone who has made a habit of dwelling on the fact that you are heard by Christ, you'll be more aware of the importance of blessing others with the gift of a listening ear. One of the most overlooked but powerful ways a person can demonstrate the heart of Christ to someone else is through his or her willingness to listen.

Strip your pride away. Sacrifice your time and mental distractions. Be quick to listen when your brother or sister selects you as the one deemed worthy of having the privilege to hear his or her words of confession, grief, sorrow, or triumph. Value the individual as Christ values you.

DWELL ON THIS

Jesus continually shows me that I'm valued. For His glory, today I will look for ways to value listening as much as I value speaking.

The issues that weigh you down today won't weigh you down forever.

> Do not lose heart. Though our outer self is wasting away, our inner self is being renewed day by day. For this light momentary affliction is preparing for us an eternal weight of glory beyond all comparison.
>
> —*2 Corinthians 4:16–17*

I have learned by experience that I'm not good at walking on crutches.

A few years after our children were born, Andrea and I bought a new house. It was an all-brick bi-level home on a uniquely shaped piece of land. The driveway was on the side of the house instead of in front like you might expect. To reach the main road, the driveway was made extra long, and a gutter was dug along the edge to help with water runoff.

One summer afternoon, I said goodbye to Andrea and the kids and started walking outside to my car. I had a few errands to run. I don't remember where I was going or what I was doing, but it certainly wasn't anything important.

As I left the house, I walked out the back door and made my way toward the driveway. It was a beautiful day, and I wasn't paying close attention to where I stepped. Without realizing what I was doing, I unintentionally stepped into the gutter, rolled my right ankle in a direction it was not meant to bend, and came crashing down onto the blacktop. In the span of one second, I had gone from casually admiring the beautiful day to lying on the ground and experiencing the worst pain I had ever felt in my life.

I writhed in anguish on the driveway. Making matters worse, the blacktop was scalding hot from the sun. I wanted to get up, but all I could do was roll back and forth while moaning out the sounds of my agony.

As I tried to wrap my mind around what had just happened, I wasn't aware that anyone else was around. But within a few moments, a man who was visiting my neighbors came running up to me. He had seen me fall and could clearly tell I was in an immense amount of pain. He told me later that he'd thought I was having a heart attack.

He offered to help me get back on my feet, but I couldn't get up—at least not at first. The pain in my ankle was so intense I was starting to feel sick to my stomach. I kept waiting for the pain to subside, but it wouldn't. As I continued to lie on the ground, I thought, *Is this pain ever going to stop?*

After a few minutes, the pain became more tolerable, and the man helped me stand. He kept me steady and let me lean on him so I could slowly limp back into my house. Andrea was shocked to see an unfamiliar man helping me walk and guiding me back into the house, where I sat on a chair and propped my leg up. He stuck around for a few minutes to make sure I was okay, then left.

Andrea took me to the hospital, where it was determined that my ankle was severely sprained. The doctor actually said, "This would have been much less painful if you had simply broken it." In the hours that followed, my ankle became very swollen, and in the following days, my leg—from my ankle to my knee—turned different shades of black, blue, purple, and yellow. It would have made a nice color palette for a painting of a sunset, if it weren't an injury.

I was given instructions on how to treat it and sent home with a soft cast and crutches. I tend to be a fast walker, so I really never adjusted to the crutches. More than once, I tried walking faster than crutches are designed to accommodate and fell flat on my face. The severity of the injury and my inability to adjust to walking on crutches made the whole ordeal feel as if it were never going to end. But, thankfully, it did. In time, my ankle healed.

Some of the hardest seasons in my life have followed a pattern similar to that injury. I've been severely and unexpectedly hurt. I've found it difficult to get up. I've needed help to get back on my feet. I've needed time to heal. But eventually I got better.

We don't get to plan our trials. They always show up at unwelcome and inopportune times. And sometimes they hit with such force that it feels as though we'll never be able to get back up again. But by the grace of God, we can learn to trust that He has better things in store for us that are still up ahead.

Most people are consumed and overburdened with temporary things that they treat like eternal matters, and maybe we frequently find ourselves in the same boat. But real life, the kind that we're granted through a relationship with Jesus, isn't temporary or transient; it's everlasting and eternal. The Holy Spirit inspired Paul to write down some rather interesting words of comfort on this subject that we should dwell on with regularity.

Paul said, "We do not lose heart. Though our outer self is wasting away, our inner self is being renewed day by day. For this light momentary affliction is preparing for us an eternal weight of glory beyond all comparison" (2 Corinthians 4:16–17). Consider what Paul was trying to help us understand in those sentences:

Do not lose heart. When we're in the midst of a heavy season of adversity and affliction, it can be easy for us to lose heart and give up. We may start preaching a message to our hearts that is the direct opposite of the hope we've been offered through Jesus. But God's will is that we would maintain a hopeful perspective. He invites us to see beyond the moment and look forward to the future He has secured for us.

Your outer self is wasting away. If my greatest hope was in the preservation of present body, this aspect of Paul's words would trouble me more than it does. It's an obvious fact of life that the human body, in its present state, wears out. The plus side of that reality, however, is that our present bodies, which are subject to the damaging effects of sin, are not fit for the sinless eternity the Lord has prepared for us. Therefore, He has promised to bless us with new, incorruptible bodies, and He's told us about it ahead of time so we can remain optimistic, even while we observe our present bodies declining.

Your inner self is being renewed daily. The Holy Spirit continues His work to produce holiness in our lives. He is transforming us. He is changing us. He is enabling us to understand things, see things, feel things, and value things that used to be hidden from us. Every day, as He does His miraculous work in our lives, we learn to see with His eyes, perceive with His mind, and feel with His heart.

Your afflictions are light and momentary. The painful trials and ordeals we endure during this season of life aren't trivialized by this truth, but they are put in their proper perspective. God invites us to think long term about all sorts of things. From the perspective of what Christ endured when He took the sin of the world upon Himself at the cross, our afflictions are light. From the perspective of eternity, our afflictions last only a short moment, and then they're over. God has given us the capacity to heal from our afflictions, and He has given us the opportunity to see beyond them.

Your afflictions are being used by the Lord to prepare you for better things ahead. The Lord isn't wasteful. He brings good from every trial, and He develops our strength, wisdom, and faith through the afflictions we face at present.

Not long ago, I was talking to my daughter Hannah about some of these very concepts, and she shared a phrase with me that I think I'll always remember. She said, "Bad things have a shelf life." I thought that was a clever statement that illustrates the deeper-level truth the Lord is trying to help us understand in His Word. Adversity spoils. Afflictions expire. Earthly sorrows remain stuck in time. They don't follow the children of God into eternity.

What's weighing you down right now? Has something painful unexpectedly come into your life? Are you weighed down with fear of the unknown? Are you grieving a loss? Are you experiencing the effects of someone else's mistakes? Are you burdened by the consequences of choices you now regret?

If so, don't lose heart. Don't become so consumed with the heaviness of your pain that you fail to see beyond it. Keep in mind that you aren't required to bear those weights alone.

Every burden feels heavier when we become convinced we're on our own to carry it. In Christ, we find help to carry our burdens. We find hope when we're losing heart. We have a compassionate Savior who hasn't abandoned us to be crushed by weights that we've mistakenly believed would be allowed to flatten us.

Don't tell yourself you'll be crushed when Christ promises you'll be renewed.

Bad things have a shelf life. The issues that weigh you down today won't weigh you down forever. Someday you'll see that, but in the meantime, give your heart permission to believe it before your eyes have the chance to catch up.

DWELL ON THIS

> Through Christ, I can see beyond this present moment. The issues that weigh me down today won't weigh me down forever.

DAY 31

You can trust God's timing to be perfect.

When the fullness of time had
come, God sent forth his Son, born
of woman, born under the law, to
redeem those who were under the
law, so that we might receive
adoption as sons.

—*Galatians 4:4–5*

The time we've been given is a fixed commodity. God has
ordained all our days. We were born at fixed times and will
take our final breaths on this earth at the precise times of His
choosing, not one day early or late.

The older I get, the more I have learned to value time. Recently, someone I respect and glean wisdom from invited me
to give him a call. I thought the call was going to be brief, but
we chatted for more than an hour. When the call was finished,
I thought, *He just carved out an hour of his life and invested it in me.* I
was grateful for that gift.

But I haven't always valued time the way I do now. In fact, I
can remember a season when I made a game out of wasting it.

When I was putting together the class schedule for my senior year of high school, I was informed that I had plenty of credits completed from previous years and could take two study halls each day if I wanted. That sounded incredibly boring to me, so I rejected that suggestion and signed up to take a course in meteorology and another one in physics. I knew I was creating extra work for myself by doing that, but it seemed better than staring at a wall for two hours a day doing nothing.

I did rather well in the meteorology class. It was taught by Joe Snedeker, an outgoing and very entertaining TV meteorologist who works at WNEP, the local ABC affiliate station in Scranton. But I didn't do quite as well in physics. There was something about that class that just didn't click with my brain.

It soon became apparent that I wasn't the only person struggling in that physics class. The content was difficult to master. Also, the class was held early in the day, and I would assume it's rather challenging for most people to wrap their minds around the nuances of that particular science first thing in the morning.

During one class, our teacher made an offhanded comment about satellite technology, even though it wasn't related to what we were studying. We all seemed interested in what he shared, so he brought it up again another day. I asked him a follow-up question about it, and he took at least fifteen minutes to answer. My friends were thrilled because the longer he talked about satellites, the less work we had to do in class.

A few days later, my good friend Sean Tierney stopped me before class to suggest something. He said, "You should see how long you can get him to talk about satellites today. See if you can make it last the entire class." I liked that idea and knew that my classmates would be appreciative if I succeeded, so I agreed to give it a try. I sat in the front of the room with the specific goal of seeing if I could get our teacher to waste the entire class period. Amazingly, it worked.

As I kept asking questions and dragging the conversation out longer and longer, the rest of the class sat silent, watching this all unfold. I desperately wanted to look at the clock so I'd know how much longer I had to go, but I didn't dare look because I didn't want to remind the teacher of how much time this conversation was eating up. When I couldn't stretch the conversation out any longer, the teacher glanced up at the clock and realized there were barely five minutes left in class. He didn't make us do any additional work that day since there wasn't enough time. Our plan worked, and throughout that day, my friends made me feel as though I had just accomplished something special. For a brief moment, I felt like the king of wasting time. Unfortunately, that came at the cost of actually learning the material our teacher was trying to help us learn.

I'm glad God isn't good at wasting time. In fact, He doesn't waste anything. He has time all mapped out and orchestrates all things in His perfect timing. He does that on a grand scale and on an individual scale.

Sometimes I have tried to get ahead of God's timing. I have attempted to rush what He wanted to gradually unfold. I have whined in prayer because I wanted to see, experience, or possess something sooner than God had planned. But when I look back over my life, I can see God's hand at work and I'm grateful for the wisdom He displays as He times everything perfectly.

Scripture speaks of God's timing in a way that comforts me. In Galatians 4, we read, "When the fullness of time had come, God sent forth his Son, born of woman, born under the law, to redeem those who were under the law, so that we might receive adoption as sons" (verses 4–5).

From the earliest pages of Scripture, we are told that the day was coming when the Savior of the world would be sent to earth. All throughout the Old Testament, we're given additional pieces of the story. We are told about the family line He would be born into. We are given glimpses of what would be taking place in world history at the time of His coming. We are told more about how He would interact with people while He was here, and we are told that His suffering and death would be barbaric.

For many generations, people wondered if they would have the privilege to be on this earth at the same time as Jesus when He fulfilled these prophecies. They wanted Him to come quickly, and they were looking forward to what Scripture revealed He would do. But Jesus didn't come to this earth a day early, and He didn't die a day too soon. When He rose from the grave on the third day after His crucifixion, He was right on time. When He ascended back to heaven forty days after His resurrection, He was honoring a divine timetable. And when He returns to this earth to rule and reign as King, His timing will remain perfect.

God sent His Son in the fullness of time, at just the right time, to rescue and redeem lost humanity. And just as this immensely consequential divine act was accomplished according to His perfect timetable, so too can we be confident that the seemingly inconsequential details of our lives occur according to the perfect timing of God. Nothing escapes His perfect plan.

You grew up where and when you did on purpose. God planned it.

You lost your first tooth on the day God ordained for that to happen.

You graduated from high school with the people God wanted you to meet at the exact time He wanted it to happen.

If you're single, embrace this season of your life as part of God's unfolding timetable for you. Your timetable doesn't have to match the life calendar of your sister or the expectations of anyone else in your life. Trust God to direct your course.

If you're waiting on children or grandchildren, understand that if it's God's will to send them to you, they won't be arriving a day early. Trust His will and His timing.

If you're waiting for a door to open, don't grow bitter or lose heart. God can't be rushed, and He can't be stopped.

If you're afraid of the future, don't feed your heart anxious thoughts. God has the whole thing mapped out. His timing is set. He will resolve every loose end and bring all things to a perfect resolution. If you have faith in Christ, you can also trust His plan to give you an incorruptible body that is fit for the new heaven and earth, where He will reign. It's all going to happen according to His schedule—not one moment early, and not a moment late.

When we, with our selfish expectations, dwell on artificial timetables of our own making, we rob ourselves of joy and contentment. God's timeline might be drastically different from what we're anticipating, but that isn't a cause for disappointment.

Christ came and rescued us in the fullness of time. When we accept that fact as true, we also have to accept that this means God had the timing of all the details that surrounded that rescue under His control as well. Logically, this would have to include the big and small things, the memorable and the mundane, the macro and the micro.

If you've been telling yourself that your life is out of order just because it doesn't match your expectations or line up with what you've observed God do in someone else's life, it's time to give yourself a break from that line of thinking. God's timetable for someone else isn't His timetable for you. That should be obvious, considering that the people you're comparing yourself to weren't born at the same exact second you were born. From the start, it was clear that you were operating on a different schedule, and that's perfectly fine. It's all part of the plan.

Take comfort in knowing that God has all things under His control.

Give yourself permission to not only accept but also rejoice over the perfection of God's timing.

The Lord's love for you is not a trivial and arbitrary thing. It means He is actively seeking only what is best for you.

His perfect timing is further evidence of His love.

DWELL ON THIS

God has a plan for my life and has all aspects of it under control. I can trust His timing to be perfect.

ACKNOWLEDGMENTS

I have many reasons to be grateful.

When writing a book, you become keenly aware that you need the help and support of those you love in order for your task to truly be a success. I'm grateful for Jesus Christ; His love, guidance, and direction; and the unique cast of characters He has brought into my life.

I'm grateful for my wife, Andrea, who goes out of her way to encourage and help me with every task I choose to commit myself to. She makes everything I do better, and the Lord reminds me daily of the blessing she is to me.

I'm grateful for my children, who make me feel loved while also keeping me on my knees in prayer. They have been on an interesting ride with Andrea and me, and we're fascinated to see the Lord's hand at work in their lives. They truly are a joy and a blessing.

I'm grateful for my agent, Jim Hart. Jim is the type of guy who genuinely has an author's best interests at heart. We clicked from day one, and the counsel he has given me as an author has been invaluable.

I'm grateful for my editor, Susan Tjaden, and the team of professionals at WaterBrook. Susan and her team have had a vision for what this book could be, and her input along the way has helped fashion this content in helpful and encouraging ways. She is a joy to work with.

I'm grateful for our church family at Core Creek Community Church. It is a privilege to worship and serve Jesus together with them. I'm also deeply appreciative of the many ways they have encouraged me as their pastor while also finding thoughtful ways to be a blessing to my wife and children.

Lastly, I'm grateful for everyone who has made investments in my life that have pointed me toward Jesus. I believe that every relationship the Lord allows us to have is on purpose. We learn from each other, we challenge each other, and we gain a greater appreciation for God's goodness through the expression of each other's gifts. If we've had the privilege to meet, I'm grateful that you are part of my life.

ABOUT THE AUTHOR

John Stange is a follower of Jesus, husband to Andrea, and father to four great kids. He holds degrees in Bible, education, and counseling; is a certified speaker, trainer, and coach with the John Maxwell Team; and serves as the lead pastor of Core Creek Community Church in Langhorne, Pennsylvania. John is an adjunct professor at Cairn University, where he teaches courses on church planting, theology, and counseling. He also serves as the director of the National Mission Board, which is a ministry that focuses on church planting and church health.

Since 1998, John has been serving in full-time Christian leadership. In 2008, he moved to Langhorne, where he worked with a team of volunteers to plant Core Creek Community Church.

John hosts three podcasts: *Chapter-A-Day Audio Bible, Daily Devotions with Pastor John,* and *Sermons, Bible Studies, and Training.* All three podcasts can be freely accessed via your favorite podcast app.

John blogs at www.desirejesus.com and would love to connect with you there. If you're interested in being among the first to be notified of his new releases, be sure to subscribe to his email list. He also regularly sends out devotions and other useful tools for spiritual growth and personal development.

Words of affirmation for your desk, nightstand, or anywhere

By nature, we prefer to walk by sight. This is universally true of all people, but walking by sight doesn't bring God glory, nor does it bring our hearts joy. As our relationship with the Lord matures, He teaches us that we can experience greater joy through walking by faith.

DWELL ON THESE THINGS
INSPIRATION CARDS

31 Thoughts to Align Your Heart with God's Truth

John Stange

Ink & Willow

Also Available Inspiration Cards

Find out more at
DesireJesus.com/DwellOnTheseThings

Ink & Willow

inkandwillow.com